an oriel incorporated publication,
bleeding edge™ group

Leadership Development

for females who went to
Catholic Grade School

Excerpt from *A Return to Love* © 1993 Marianne Williamson used with permission. (NY: HarperCollins, pp. 188-189.)

Excerpt from *High Flyers* © 1998 The President and Fellows of Harvard University used with permission. (Morgan W. McCall, Jr., *High Flyers.* Boston: Harvard Business School Press, pp. 62-63.)

3800 Regent Street   P.O. Box 5445   Madison, WI 53705-0445   USA
www.orielinc.com

1-800-669-8326 or 608-238-8134

First printing, August 1998

Leadership Development

Development

for females who went to

Catholic Grade School

Oriel™

an oriel incorporated publication,
bleeding edge™ group

iv

You received
our dear Lord in

First Holy Communion

on *November 25* 19*72*

in *St. John Vianney* Church

from the Reverend
Schmelzer

You were then *8*
years old

Development Team

Jeanne Dosch Editor	Vickie Peters Production
Jan Harris Design and Desktop Publishing	Angela Prestil Project Manager
Eric Hummel Subject Matter Expert	Angela Schoeneck Product Manager/Marketing
Dale Mann Illustrator	Franny VanNevel Writer and Subject Matter Expert
Jennifer Olski Proofreader	Patricia Zander Subject Matter Expert

Credits and Acknowledgements

There were numerous people who helped guide the development of this book. Many freely shared their stories and knowledge of the Catholic religion, and many reviewed and provided feedback on our writings. You were wonderful to be so open and helpful to us. Contributors include: Nancy Buechel, Sandra Custer, Sue Derhammer, Kasey DeWitt, Mary Dwyer, Susan Fischer, Kelli Frankenberg, Casey Garhart, Nancy Hadley, Pat Heim, Julie Herfel, Sandra Hoard, Beth Ingels, Sr. Elizabeth McAuliffe, Sr. Winifred Morgan, Ann Myers, Sr. Margaret O'Brien, Pat Palleschi, Sue Reynard, Stephanie Roahen, Debi Ruckert, Sheriene Saadati, Roseanne Saunders, Judy Schector, Lori Silverman, Barbara Streibel, Lisa Strub, Mary Stultz, Mary Wagner, and Rose Zoppa.

foreword

Not only am I a "product" of Catholic grade school, but also Catholic high school and Catholic college. That's 16 years of Catholic education!! The plot thickens. I am also a Sister of Mercy whose life has been spent in Catholic elementary, high school, and university teaching and administration. I suspect those credentials had something to do with being asked to write this foreward. (Would that it had been for my literary prowess!)

What the authors did not know when they asked me to comment on this book was that I was expelled from the first grade—for talking! Isn't that what six- and seven-year-olds do best? I guess Sister had other ideas. (A side note, the boy I was talking with was not even reprimanded! But that is grist for another mill.) After my mother "conferenced" with the pastor of the parish, I was readmitted. Despite my early trauma, I learned how to read and write in that very same classroom. The good news is that I have enjoyed telling that story for years. As an adult I can look back and smile.

Like many who are quoted in this book, I enjoyed my Catholic grade school education. Yes, there were situations that were less than admirable, but through it all I learned to love learning, to be curious, to voice my opinion, and to value my faith. For whatever reason, I was able to separate the less important elements of my grade school years from the more important. The Sisters nurtured a religious vocation within me. They were supportive, challenging and faithful.

The women with whom I now share community recognized my leadership potential. They fostered it and encouraged me to develop it. They are among my most significant mentors. They taught me the "SIPOC Method" without even knowing it. Throughout my 31 years in education, I have had both Catholic school and public school experience. I have watched as teachers used their classrooms as mini-leadership development courses.

In this book, the authors touch a live nerve in many of us. They explore the impact of past experiences on our present and future development. Often this is done through humor. Throughout, they remind us that if we are reading this book there is a leader lurking within us, just screaming to come out. They are saying the same thing to us that Sister said: "You can do whatever you set your mind to!"

The challenge of this book is to reflect on our past and to evaluate it with the wisdom and understanding that we have gained in the process of becoming women. This book has the potential to make you smile, make you angry, and make you grateful. More importantly, it has the potential to make you into the leader you want to become.

Elizabeth A. McAuliffe, RSM, Ed. D.
President, St. Mary Academy-Bay View
Riverside, Rhode Island

Dedication

This book is dedicated to all women and men who have the courage, humility, and passion to become leaders, for they are overcoming many odds and are sharing their light so others can learn to shine.

Table of *Contents*

Introduction

Why would a management consulting firm with a strong background in implementing data-based decision making and process management write and publish this book? Precisely because our professional experience has taught us the complexity of the issues faced in business today and the importance of leadership.

It is because of this recognition of the need for leadership that this book was conceived. Looking at my own leadership role as well as those of executives I have worked with in other corporations, it became clear that the biggest challenges were rarely limited to the business issues. They often occurred at a much deeper character level, the source of true leadership.

Your leadership style and ability are profoundly influenced by who you are. Who you are is related to your own personal history. This book is about making behavior changes that are based on understanding yourself and challenging your learnings and beliefs in order to develop your own leadership style. For many, this means extracting the good, discarding the not so good, and trying again. For me, moving ahead and "getting over it" means I can laugh about it.

The Catholic grade school experience is only one example of an early learning experience; of course there are many others and you have your own unique background. The real message is that as a leader, you must continually work to develop yourself. Within these pages we describe a strategy and methodology for doing that.

Although I conceived the idea for this book based on my own experiences, it would not have been possible without the expertise and assistance of some key players. As with all Oriel Incorporated projects, it began by pulling a team of individuals together to work on the book. The team was made up of a variety of women who had attended Catholic grade school and one "Public." Franny VanNevel wrote the first complete draft of the book, and also contributed many of the stories from her years growing up in Catholic grade school. Dr. Eric Hummel provided the leadership content, as well as offering his expertise at focusing on the positives from our grade school years.

We had the pleasure and great fortune to speak with and learn from many women about their Catholic education experiences. In Chapter 10, you will read personal testaments that will remind many of you of your own memorable experiences. (We would be remiss if we did not acknowledge that some things have changed within Catholic grade schools since many of us experienced them.) While we have many stories and experiences in common, we each have our unique perspective. It is our honor to share our stories and our book with you. I hope you will finish it with an increased understanding of leadership development and a smile on your face.

Patricia Zander, CEO/Owner
Oriel Incorporated

Part 1

Catholic Girls Start Much Too Late

Chapter 1

The Leadership Journey: Twisted Sisters

• • • • •

*T*his book is about a very important journey. It's a journey of continually improving your leadership abilities so you can enjoy your efforts today, be a shining star in the future, and reap the benefits of your Catholic grade school education. Excuse me, did I hear you right? What does Catholic grade school have to do with anything? Well, first of all, you're already ignoring your *true calling*, which is to be a nun. Don't try to worm your way out of it. Remember vocation day? The only *real* choice was to figure out which order of nuns to join; any other job was merely an avocation. And, as Sister Mary Fill-In-The-Blank warned, the punishment is worse for those who hear the call and ignore it. Think about where you are today. Was Sister right? However, if you're already a nun you're off the hook. Unless, of course, you're coveting the job of Mother Superior, then you're just a plain old sinner like the rest of us. Go say three Hail Marys in the corner.

The process of becoming (and being) a leader is like eternity—there's really no end. True leaders never stop learning and growing. Hopefully, we'll limit this to *inward* growth and leave our thighs out of it. If you're like most leaders, you'll find equal amounts of heaven and hell in this loop.

Becoming a leader is a bit like becoming a saint. You have to suffer, perform a few documented miracles, and never lose your faith. As did the saints, you'll face throngs of people just itching to cast stones at you and rail to the powers that be that you're not worthy. But, when it comes right down to it, who *is* worthy? Sometimes we get lucky, sometimes we get there by grit, and sometimes grit is thrust upon us. Take Mary Dwyer as she shares a glimpse of her journey to leadership:

> *Sometimes you're the windshield, sometimes you're the bug.*
> Mark Knopfler
> Songwriter

I believe it was by accident for me. My first goal in my work life was to work hard at a decent job and if I could do that it was fine. I never had very high aspirations other than to do whatever I did do very well. By doing it very well I did move along and I did advance myself. But it's not because I woke up and said, "By the time I'm 25 I'm going to be at this level in this company." That was too aspirational. You know, you have to keep yourself down a little bit, which goes back to what we were taught—"don't think too highly of yourself." But in retrospect I think I am where I am today because of my religious upbringing and my parent's discipline. In a very kind of quiet way they encouraged us to achieve.

Mary Dwyer, Vice President/Accounts Supervisor
Lindsay, Stone & Briggs Advertising Incorporated

But my therapist said...

You're probably wondering why anyone would create a leadership development book specifically for females who went to Catholic grade school. Why, in God's holy name, would we do that to you when you've already paid big bucks to a therapist to help you get over this very same experience? Pat P. takes us back to her grade school days:

> My overwhelming remembrance of going to grade school in Brooklyn—and I just went to the first three grades—is anxiety. We would be put in rows according to our capability and the rows would change every week. I remember throwing up on Monday mornings on the way to school because I was so nervous about where I would be placed. I think it made me anal retentive because it was a very circumscribed life.
>
> Pat P., VP of HRD
> Fortune 100 company

Here's our promise (no fingers crossed): This journey is not one which you'll have to suffer through while offering up your pain to the poor souls in purgatory. Well, okay, there might be a *little* suffering, but the soul you'll be freeing is your own.

In case you're starting to wonder, this is not a "find yourself" book. Good Catholic girls aren't into finding themselves, they're into losing themselves in prayer and service. This book will focus on the elements and processes that will help you become a better leader. As we go through this process, we hope to take that innocent, little Catholic girl who lives inside you (whether practicing or recovering) and turn her into the patron saint of all employees—*A Great Leader*.

As we're sure you discovered in those expensive counseling sessions, our early learning experiences color our views of the world. Many of us came out of Catholic grade school wearing rose-colored glasses. But we should have been issued machine shop goggles. The world is a dangerous place for innocents. Any female who went to Catholic grade school and studied under the watchful eye of God and Sister Mary Margaret Maria Theresa Catherine can immediately bond with another of her kind. Even though everyone's experience was unique, as sisters-in-Catholicism we're all identical twins. You get what we mean.

We're assuming that being raised and educated Catholic contained some rather extreme elements for all of us. If it didn't for you, drop down on your knees and give thanks to God that you escaped unscathed. While you're at it, say a prayer for those of us who still have nightmares about Sr. Michael Damien.

Come on...it won't hurt (much)

We're not here to bash Catholicism, we just want to tweak its nose a little. We want to help you explore the impact a Catholic grade school education had and continues to have on you. After we laugh about it, understand it, and accept it, this book will help you learn how to leverage the positives and deep six the negatives to become a better leader. Are you confused? Well, let's look at it this way—if you're tempted to pin a chapel veil to your hair before you enter the boss's office, that's a negative. Untie the Catholic knots and you'll find you have a healthy respect for authority, which can be a positive.

Think back to Catholic grade school. Yes, open that tightly closed door and dare to peek through. We were so immersed in the teaching and rituals that we couldn't comprehend the existence of another world. (At least not until we were older and skipped class to watch *Another World*. But that's another story.) Because the scope of our world was so limited, we didn't understand that we were different or how we were different. We were the normal ones and *they* were all different. It was essentially *Us* versus *The Publics*, which included everyone who went to public school. Since we believed we were the only ones going to heaven, any further distinctions were meaningless.

Once you enter the workplace, you find yourself on yet another closed set. Each organization has its unique belief system, its rituals, and its commandments. And consciously or not, you'll find yourself reverting to some old Catholic behaviors and beliefs in the business environment. It's a natural reaction.

So grab your rosary, straighten your scapular, and polish those patent leather shoes. We're going for it. Hey, what have you got to lose? (Remember, leave your thighs out of this!) Besides becoming an extraordinarily gifted leader, making this trip will grant you a plenary indulgence.

A sobering thought: What if, right at this very moment, I am living up to my full potential?

Jane Wagner
Author

Chapter 2

The Leadership Role:
Nun of the Above

• • • • •

Our deepest fear is not that we are inadequate.
Our deepest fear is that we are powerful beyond measure.
It is our light, not our darkness, that frightens us.

We ask ourselves, who am I to be brilliant, gorgeous, talented and fabulous?
Actually, who are you not to be?
You are a child of God.
Your playing small doesn't serve the world.
There's nothing enlightened about shrinking so that other people won't feel insecure around you.

We were born to manifest the glory of God within us.
It's not just in some of us; it's in everyone.
And as we let our light shine, we unconsciously give other people permission to do the same.
As we are liberated from our own fear, our presence automatically liberates others.

Marianne Williamson
A Return to Love

Leaders dream. They can touch and taste a vision, and they inspire others to follow. They reach deep within themselves to bring out the best, and encourage those around them to do the same. We are here together on a journey of learning and change. You are here as a leader striving to learn better ways to develop your own unique leadership style and abilities. You will find that your true character will be the artist and guide of your vision. You must *trust* yourself, have faith in your dream, and be driven by your passion.

There are good and bad leaders, and there are good and bad visions. Some leaders inspire and their followers go higher. Other leaders inspire and their followers expire. You are here to learn how you can give others the opportunity and permission to shine. You are here to learn how to take that rare piece of art that is you, and to share all of its power and beauty with those around you. Once you've realized your own potential, we'll help you learn to inspire others to lead.

The perfect leader...is she lurking inside you?

We all seem to start at the same point on the leadership development journey as we search for the one true definition of leadership or the perfect role model. You remember your patron saint, don't you? As with everything else, accomplishing something valuable and special is never easy, and to make it more difficult, leadership trends keep coming and going. They keep us spinning in circles. Hero today, goner tomorrow. In reality, things change, ideas change, times change, and, hopefully, so does your hairdo.

So what are we supposed to make of all this? Remember this—some things do remain the same. Leadership isn't about fads or gimmicks and it's certainly not about lipstick color, business suits with high heels, or flashy business trends. It goes much deeper and it's more genuine. It's honest, real, and sincere, and your true leadership abilities can only come from you, a unique individual.

Pass the roles, please

As a leader you will play many different roles. You won't always be a hero, out ahead of everybody else. In fact, sometimes you may be most helpful as you bring up the rear. But don't look at leadership like a parade; look at it like *The Stroll*. You remember that old dance—the original line dance—where each person got a turn to strut his or her stuff down the center of two rows of dancers.

There is no single definition of leadership; there are hundreds. They vary because they identify the essence of leadership from different perspectives—from the follower's point of view, the

> *We can't all be heroes. Somebody has to sit on the curb and clap as they go by.*
>
> Will Rogers

> *To lead the people, walk behind them.*
>
> Lao-tzu

results point of view, the organizational role, and the character point of view. Successful leaders learn to operate from all these perspectives. Susan Fischer gives her perspective:

> I think it's a combination of personality and experiences and taking advantage of opportunities. I'm not a goal-driven person but I do tend to look for opportunities. I took advantage of opportunities. When a situation comes up and no one else is jumping in, I jump in.
>
> Susan Fischer, Assistant Director of Financial Aid
> University of Wisconsin-Madison

Our definition of a leader is very simple:

Someone who is on a path, in quest of a goal, and who behaves in a way that motivates others to follow and join in the leading.

It had long since come to my attention that people of accomplishment rarely sat back and let things happen to them. They went out and happened to things.

Elinor Smith
1920s pioneering
female pilot

Now we can move on to working on one of the most critical elements: helping you determine how to become that special "someone." There are many characteristics that successful leaders share. One of the most important requirements of leadership is to understand your own style and your own way of making it happen. We're talking about authentic leadership—the real deal. There are many characteristics that successful leaders share. For example, we can agree that leaders have to be supportive yet firm, but we can't say how you, in your personal style, will exhibit this.

Common characteristics of leaders

- Leaders often seem to be presented with or create challenging opportunities to change, grow, innovate, and improve. They never leave a task, job, or position the same way they found it. Because of this, the results often exceed original expectations.

- Leaders not only happen to things, they happen to themselves. The need for growth and change is in their soul. Leaders don't wait for the seeds to fall. They plant them. They take responsibility for their own growth and development every day.

- Leaders project honesty, and through their honesty and consistency they engender trust.

- Leaders embody passion. They are a fundamental source of energy for those around them.

- Leaders are advocates. They are promoters of people, of change, of values, of the mission, and of the processes.

- Leaders are more than communicators. They carry the message visibly and audibly, as an Olympic athlete would carry the torch.

- Leaders intimately know fear, humility, and self-doubt. They also know how to lead in the face of these daunting emotions.

- Leaders practice self-reflection. They also interact with others who provide them honest feedback, and they are open to learning.

- Leaders are able to link self-knowledge and business knowledge with the goals of the organization.

- Leaders behave with urgency, competency, and integrity.

- Leaders value profit, not for its own sake, but for its ability to sustain growth for long-standing success.

- Leaders know ongoing change is unavoidable. They excite others about change and implement change faster than the competition.

- Leaders know when to take charge, and when and how to empower others. They influence the environment in a way that helps others achieve success.
- Leaders understand that speed is a critical competitive advantage. They know their ability to respond rapidly and think quickly is vital. Speed in decision making often requires making decisions at the character level.
- Leaders are always searching for new ideas, and they are creative. They demand innovation and learning from themselves and others in order to realize the vision.
- Leaders embrace the responsibility to develop others. They are the stewards of the organization with the mission of ensuring constant renewal and growth of leadership at all levels.
- Leaders are resilient. They persevere.

This may seem overwhelming. As a Catholic grade school graduate you take the role of being a leader very seriously. It is an awesome challenge. In fact, it's almost saintly. At the same time, you carry around the oh-so-common Catholic self-doubt. This can be a challenging mix. Don't despair, we'll push on together.

> *The time when you need to do something is when no one else is willing to do it, when people are saying it can't be done.*
>
> Mary Frances Berry
> Chair, Civil Rights Commission

Okay, so I have the recipe...do I have the ingredients?

We've just reviewed the list of important attributes of a successful leader, so we should be able to take a dab of this and a pinch of that and come up with the perfect leader, right? We wish. There is no one recipe, no single magic list of skills or competencies to master. We can't even give you a rundown of what innate talents you need to become a crackerjack leader. But if you are here reading this book, it's in you. We're going to help you take hold of your experiences, your beliefs, and your ability to learn and adapt. By doing so, you'll be able to nurture your potential and grow it into effective leadership behaviors.

It's human nature to look for solutions outside ourselves. It always seems easier to fix someone or something else. We rarely think of using introspection and changing ourselves. As a result, we often try to change things over which we have little control. The trick is to learn that the answers are most likely within us. Now for the good news: you alone are responsible for becoming the kind of leader you envision. The bad news: you alone are responsible for becoming the kind of leader you envision. Ugh! Why is it always up to us?

It's not so bad. As a leader, you are truly in an enviable situation. Your most powerful tools are your attitude and commitment. Both are completely under your control.

If you don't like the way I drive, stay off the sidewalk

The type of leader you become will directly affect your organization. A leader's sense of purpose, conviction, ethics, professionalism, and assertion are reflected in the organizational culture. A leader's effectiveness provides the foundation for the organization, and this foundation becomes the future. Imagine, you are in command of the essential tools for making this happen. And you can enhance and hone those tools as often as you like, to whatever level of excellence you choose.

Ultimately, the type of leader you become depends on your ability to fully develop your leadership style and skills. Your attitude and commitment are the keys. You are ready for the first step of the journey if you are willing to:

- ❏ Accept your desire to be a leader
- ❏ Challenge your attitude and develop a new mindset
- ❏ Seek knowledge whenever and wherever possible
- ❏ Learn how to successfully translate knowledge into behavior
- ❏ Try out new behaviors
- ❏ Proactively obtain and evaluate feedback
- ❏ Practice, modify, and expand your new behaviors
- ❏ Transfer your knowledge freely to the organization

If you can honestly check off every readiness factor on this list, you are ready. If not, do you understand why an item is a challenge for you? Can you set it aside for now? Note your problem areas and remember them for later reference. You will have plenty of opportunity to face them as we go along.

A funny thing happened on the way to...

You never know when or where you'll be when you learn something essential. In writing this book, the first time we pondered the concepts of managing and leading, we also reflected on what it takes to maintain employee motivation and productivity. We realized that these have a lot to do with leadership training, but a colleague looking in the mirror at herself came to this realization quite differently:

I was a product manager and had just resigned. I went to meet with the CEO to discuss my leaving. To my surprise, he had done some homework. He had talked to people I worked with, especially with the outside sales force I supported. He already had a feel for who was walking in the door, way before I arrived. We talked about why I was leaving, some of my frustrations, and some of his beliefs. At the end of our meeting he completely blew me away with two simple questions: What kind of employee do you think you are? How easy do you think you are to manage?

I was shocked. It had to be obvious. (After all, you can spot a good Catholic girl from miles away.) I was hardworking, self-motivated, eager to learn, extremely loyal, had very high ethics, and customer focus was my life. I had to be the dream employee for any manager. I told him what I thought. He smiled and said, "Think about the manage part."

My identity was so shaken, I had to get answers. I went to the director of sales and told him the story. He knew my work and knew me very well. Surely he would put my mind at ease. Instead he laughed and said, "You are a manager's worst nightmare. You are completely unmanageable." (Especially in situations where my manager's actions weren't consistent with the beliefs and values of the organization.) I was horrified! Me? But very quickly I began to realize they were absolutely right. Why? I was completely unmanageable in their eyes, but I could be led and I would lead if needed.

Patricia Zander, CEO/Owner
Oriel Incorporated

Isn't it ironic that the biggest leap you can make in understanding leadership is in understanding how challenging it is for someone to manage you? Patricia's experience teaches more about working with and leading people than any other experience. It illustrates the difference between managing and leading. It shows how important it is for a leader to be flexible so she can lead many different types of people. It also indicates that working with highly motivated and independent people can be the biggest challenge a leader may face. Motivated from within, independent thinkers often challenge the status quo on a regular basis. Experience, talent, and knowledge can easily be lost to the organization if people are not allowed to grow and flourish while skillfully guided.

So in the great call for leaders, some will fulfill the dream of a lifetime, some will rise to the occasion, and some will run for the nearest restroom or refrigerator. (Depending on your unique style!) No matter what the case, we are here to learn how we can continually ascend the leadership development ladder.

The Feast of St. Thigh-Master®

It's time for some exercises called Genuflections. No, we're not getting back to our thighs—these exercises aren't a form of deep knee bends. They offer you the chance to stop and take a look inside your *genuine* self and *reflect* on what you see. Hence the name Genuflections. Clever, huh? And since we all know that you, having once been a good Catholic girl, can't pass up an opportunity to do a little extra credit work on the side, we've included some templates at the back of the book to help you work through these exercises and keep track of your progress.

Genuflection

Because you're ultimately responsible for becoming the kind of leader you envision, let's start by reflecting on how swell you are. You can either write your answers right here in the book, use the templates in the Appendix, or start a journal.

What are your best qualities?

What qualities do you least like about yourself?

How will your best qualities *help* you as a leader?

How will your least desirable qualities *hinder* you as a leader?

Who are your "Patron Saints" of work? What do you admire or appreciate about them?

Imagine you are the CEO. One of your key executives is *you* as you are today. How would you as the CEO go about leading *you*? What would it be like to work with *you*?

Benediction

Go in peace. (Not panic.) And remember, you are not alone. You have many champions.

Chapter 3
Leadership Potential: Follow the Glow-in-the-Dark Rosary

• • • • •

efore we delve deeper into the key elements of leadership development, let's reflect on the importance of your role as a leader and the importance of making your own development a priority.

You can have a tremendous impact on the organization. Every day executives, managers, and leaders underestimate their own impact, be it positive or negative. The best leaders are keenly aware of the impression they make through their own personal leadership and management skills. They understand that the philosophy of customer focus travels throughout the organization and infuses each employee. They appreciate the importance of digging deep enough into issues to understand the whole truth, the value of clear and timely decision making, and the importance of making others' goals equally significant to their own. Leaders also understand that knowledge is power, yet they don't harbor it for their own advancement. Instead, they encourage everyone in the organization to seek and share knowledge. True leaders model these behaviors with passion. And most of all, they deeply understand that their development and that of others is vital for the organization's long-term viability and success. They know their development must be deliberate. Growth can't just "happen."

I want it... at least, I think I want it... Am I being too wickedly self-promoting? Is this a sin? I'll do the penance— I REALLY WANT IT! ooO

In this book, leadership development consists of an ongoing plan of continual learning and behavior change. It is based on proven models of change which are meant to bring about real, lasting, and positive transformations in your behavior and character.

Oh when the saints...

So what's required for true leadership development? When we were young Catholic girls we wanted to be saints. Saints weren't just meek little souls. They had guts, they took risks, they held strongly to their beliefs. At work you absorb the corporate war stories and you're enthralled by tales of mythical figures who climbed up the ranks to coveted leadership positions. You find a hero to emulate or a sinner to shun.

This on-the-job discovery of what's involved in becoming a leader parallels the process of your early Catholic education. It may not have seemed like a process when you were in Catholic grade school, but don't be fooled. It was formal and structured. It was a methodical journey, step-by-step, prayer-by-prayer, May Crowning-by-May Crowning, all designed to create the "perfect" Catholic girl. Leadership development isn't nearly as rigid—we really aren't into crowns, vestments, and the liberal use of holy water—but it does require some degree of formality and structure.

In those formative Catholic schoolgirl years we were obsessed with one fear—burning in hell. As women in the work force, we're obsessed with one fear—turning to Jell-O®. And we're not talking about eating too much chocolate pudding after a hard day at the office. (Although it may qualify as another obsession.) It's very simple. We really don't want to fail. To overcome this fear we believed that if we worked really hard at being good (or at least invisible), we'd be okay. That seems easy. Except what is the definition of "being good"?

As young Catholic girls, we were taught to strive for goodness at all times. Goodness meant choosing the right path for your life— both spiritual and corporeal. You could be a nun (career path), or you could be like the Blessed Mother (the at-home mom) but preferably with about 12 more kids. The saving grace was that you weren't supposed to do both at the same time. So, no matter which route you chose, the learning and development path was clear. Life seemed manageable; there was clear focus and purpose.

We've come a long way, baby
(And we're really getting tired)

But times changed. When we reached adulthood we ran headfirst into the new reality. Women's liberation opened new paths for us to follow, but there was a steep cost for all this opportunity and freedom. Now we had to do it all. Well, almost. We still weren't expected to be nuns and moms at the same time. But it was looking like being a mom and bringing home some of the bacon were both definitely in the picture. Our Catholic training didn't prepare us to prioritize the needs of our families and our jobs. In fact, now the job was a need of the family. We had learned to be all-giving. We didn't know how to say "no" to these competing callings. So many of us took on both callings eagerly, joyfully, and passionately. Hey, we were good. We had the desire, the attitude, and the commitment. We were ready to become whatever we needed to be. The troubles soon followed. A Catholic grade school graduate shares her story:

> *I am only one, but I am still one. I cannot do everything, but I can still do something. And because I cannot do everything, I will not refuse to do the something I can do.*
>
> Edward Everett Hale
> Author

> I started to realize I was in serious trouble in graduate school. I had three young children at this point. I went to my university classes at night so I could avoid getting babysitters; after all, my place was primarily in the home—oh, and in preparing for a meaningful career. Well, I had a really big test coming up the night after Halloween. I couldn't believe it—didn't they know that was very bad timing? When we got our tests back there was a

wide spread in the grades, so when our professor handed back the tests he decided to have a brief group discussion on how people had studied. Oh my goodness, what an eye opener. He went around the room, one by one. Fellow students talked about the papers they read, the hours of research in the library, the study groups they had formed. When it was my turn I said, "I finished the devil costume for the 2-year-old, the ballerina costume for the 4-year-old, and the E.T. costume for the 6-year-old, but I thought a lot about your lectures while I was sewing." The room fell silent, throats cleared and my professor changed the topic. I began to understand what was really required to be *good*, and fear of failure (and the accompanying guilt) began to raise its ugly head.

Patricia Zander, CEO/Owner
Oriel Incorporated

I, _____, take myself, to have and to hold...

Now a new dimension has been added: leadership. Is there no end to this madness? And, of course, the fear of failure isn't enough to dampen your desire to become a leader—you are answering a calling. Does this ring a bell? You don't know if you can ever reach your goal, but you want to learn more about it. You start to feel the pull. There's a building desire in you to become more, one of the chosen few. Stop! Time out! Let's put it all in perspective. This isn't career day at St. Mary's School—you don't have to prostrate yourself on the altar and commit to becoming the bride of Christ. You're not getting married, you're not even going steady yet. It's more like a crush. You're just starting to want to unleash the leadership potential inside you. But remember, what you want to accomplish is not easy. You are in a world that holds wild expectations for you, and because you are a grown-up Catholic girl you hold even higher ones for yourself.

You are now entering into a relationship with someone you can sleep with but whom you may never measure up to: your inner self. Along with this pull to lead, there's usually an equal push: the overwhelming desire to break it off. You're tempted to go hide under your desk or run away. You're afraid that you don't really get it, you don't know what you're doing. Who are you trying to kid? And worst of all, what happens if you really make it? What if people you care about actually start to follow you? What on earth do you think you're doing? You faker, you!

Everybody is ignorant, only on different subjects.

Will Rogers

I think I'm just faking it now. Sometimes people will find out that I don't know as much as they think I know or they ask me for my opinion and I kind of look around the room and figure they must be asking someone else. At my current job they treated me like I must know everything. At first it felt uncomfortable, and then I just kind of settled into it. They treat me like a "vice-president," whatever that is. I try to be human. You know it's not that I'm stepping out of the role of VP and becoming human, it's that I am [human] all the time and they just think it's so wonderful that I'm not acting like a VP.

Pat P., VP of HRD
Fortune 100 company

Nobody knows it all, and if they do, nobody wants to know them. It's okay to be scared. If you're not scared, then we're scared for you. Every step forward comes with a fresh set of fears and new things to learn. That's what development and change are all about. The important thing is not to be scared stiff. You still need to be able to function—that's always a plus.

Whether you've been captivated by the opportunity to lead, or you see the void and feel compelled to jump in and lead (God's will), you feel you have to do something. The desire is there. And while you may not know exactly what to do, you do your best. It may feel like you're faking it, but you're not. You just need to psych yourself up to perform. Hey, men have been doing it for years. It's part of doing the job.

> *Uncertainty will always be part of the taking-charge process.*
>
> John J. Gabarro
> *The Dynamics of Taking Charge*

> Part of me sees leadership as a task that needs to be done because nobody else wants to do it, so it's another burden that you take on. And then you try to work yourself harder than everyone else because that's what you're supposed to be doing.
>
> Pat P., VP of HRD
> Fortune 100 company

Keepin' the faith

Don't worry. Have faith that the ability to succeed is in you. Dare to follow your desire (or calling) to become a better leader. Don't listen to those who underestimate your identity. Add desire to your list of callings, but appreciate what you're asking of yourself. As Catholic girls, we learned how to have faith in things we couldn't see or touch. It's now time to have that faith in the power within you.

As an undergraduate I was registering for classes at the university. It was a time before computer registration so you had to go from building to building, all across the campus to sign up for classes. It was August and it was hot. Of course all the first choices were filled so I had to backtrack and re-invent my schedule after every stop. I had two small children (one on my back in a carrier and one in a stroller) and was expecting a third. Yes, my belly button was protruding, and it sent the sorority girls fleeing for fear it was contagious.

Whether you think that you can or that you can't, you're usually right.

Henry Ford

I had decided to take my first women's studies course. I was sure I would find kindred spirits. I went to the little table to register, and a liberal-looking 50-ish woman was there. She told me I couldn't sign up for the course I wanted because I didn't have the prerequisites. I told her I did, but they were taken in the science department, not through women's studies. She slowly and wisely shook her head saying that wouldn't do because women's studies courses had a deeper perspective on the issues. Then she looked me in the eyes and said, "Do you even know what it is like to be a woman of the eighties?" I kept the faith, looked her in the eyes, pointed my belly button right at her forehead and demanded, "Sign me up now!" She did. I was an "A" student.

Patricia Zander, CEO/Owner
Oriel Incorporated

Genuflection

It's time for a little bit of self-revelation. Remember "the film" we all had to see in fourth grade…no boys allowed, windows tightly shut and blinds drawn? Well, we're not going to reveal that much, thank God! But put yourself back in your formative years of Catholic grade school. Can you see yourself in your plaid jumper, white shirt, white knee socks, and saddle shoes? Good! Now don't lose that image and complete the following sentences with the first thing that pops into that little pony-tailed head of yours:

In grade school, my favorite nun was _____ because she…

If I had told my fourth grade teacher I was going to grow up to be an important leader at work she would have thought…

The first time I was a leader was when I…

In grade school, I was disappointed when I wasn't asked to lead…

Benediction

It takes courage to chart a path for your own growth and development. You may find the biggest benefit is in the harnessing and display of this courage.

Part 2

40 Days to Get Unbent

Chapter 4

Challenging Beliefs: Suffering Makes You Grow, Which is Why I'm a Size 18

• • • • •

n Chapter 2, we discussed the concept of your desire to become a better leader than you are today and every day hereafter. Well, we've also learned desire isn't enough. (Remember, the spirit is willing but the flesh is weak!) You have to learn to challenge your mindset or your attitude. This is critical because your mindset, more than anything, is what's going to determine what you can accomplish.

If you think something outside of yourself is the cause of your problem, you will look outside of yourself for the answer.

Edward Bales
Motorola University

Mindset *(mind´set´) n. A mental disposition or attitude that predetermines one's responses to and interpretations of situations.*

Webster's Dictionary

She's got a ticket to ride

In Catholic grade school we were taught that our ticket to heaven was more easily earned when the individual served God through unquestioning belief, suffering, sacrifice, and hard work. In other words, no pain, no gain. Since the major result of all this—getting into heaven—was something we had to take on faith, we didn't discuss concrete results. Instead, the true measure of excellence (while you were still alive) was whether or not your devotion and pain was deep enough. That was our source of credibility and value.

In the workplace, it's just the opposite. They expect results. But do you still get hung up on the belief that if you don't somehow suffer for the cause then you have not done your part? Be honest. This in itself is enough to load anyone down. But if you also believe that achieving the results is critical, you are heading for trouble. Add it up. The load gets pretty heavy when your criterion for a good effort is achieving the results, with a healthy schmear of suffering spread on top.

Test yourself. If your work produced a great result, but your efforts didn't seem overwhelmingly difficult, are you likely to brush off praise by saying, "It was nothing," or "I was just lucky"? Bad girl. This is a mindset that needs challenging. And the sooner the better. How are you supposed to continue to grow and reach higher levels with this ball and chain? Unfortunately, you're not alone. This mindset isn't all that unusual for a homegrown Catholic grade school girl.

Your way out is to gain an understanding of what core beliefs your mindset is based on. Then challenge those beliefs. Let's try again. Is it okay to feel proud of achieving results even when it seemed easy? Believe it or not, many people, including most men who went to Catholic grade schools, would say yes.

In a sacrificial jam

When you challenge a belief, you may be amazed at how illogical or severe it is. Or your challenge may temper and strengthen it. Even if you find a belief to be illogical, it still isn't easy to discard it. You know it's crazy, but for some reason you still hang on to it deep down and can't give it up. After all, what kind of self-serving monster would you turn into if you believed you were worthy?

> *We're not worthy.*
> Wayne and Garth

Relax, don't beat your breast and run down the church aisle over this. We spent years in a homogeneous environment where we were taught never to challenge our beliefs. In essence, we were taught not to think. Girls who didn't believe wouldn't achieve heaven. The tenants of our faith represented the one and only way. As a result we didn't gain the experience of challenging our mindsets. (Wouldn't that constitute a serious slip of faith?) Well, we may be starting late but the

> *We don't see things as they are, we see them as we are.*
> Anaïs Nin
> Author

good news is Sister Mary Theresa Catherine was right about one thing: Practice makes perfect. So practice challenging a little, let it settle, and come back later for more. And by the way, you will find it's not about giving up core beliefs, it's about reframing them from the positive perspective. By doing this, you may find that these beliefs are your biggest assets.

As a leader, the basis of your new mindset must be the belief that you are inherently good and that you have the opportunity and capability to have a tremendous positive impact on the organization. We know you have been taught some things that fly in the face of this, but trust us (and yourself) enough to give this a whirl.

To begin, we will work through some examples. After that, challenge away on your own. In order to see what it means to challenge and restructure your beliefs, we have picked some Catholic beliefs that you need to deal with in order to create your new mindset. For most of us, these teachings had a major impact on our views and attitudes about ourselves. After we challenge them, we'll begin to build a more positive perspective.

But first a warning. You might feel like a heretic—who are you to challenge these truths? Whether you feel a tug at your heart, a sense of loss, betrayal, or anger, remember these are normal reactions when you are digging down deep and challenging your core beliefs.

Challenging Your Beliefs

#1   Original sin...What a bad apple

How original is original sin when we didn't even get to commit it? This is one of the hardest things about being Catholic. We come into the world tarnished because Adam couldn't keep his mouth shut when Eve offered him the apple. She didn't want it. She was holding out for chocolate.

For this they were tossed out of paradise and as a result we were born with an indelible mark on our souls. Right out of the chute and we are already less than perfect. And if one had the misfortune to die before baptism, she'd skip heaven and trip the light fantastic to limbo for eternity!

The other bad part about original sin was that it made us more prone to evil even after we were baptized. Strike Two! Not only were we born bad, but we were going to get *badder*. And, even after Baptism, if we had the bad luck to die with an unconfessed or unrepented mortal sin on our soul, we'd go straight to hell— no matter how good we'd been otherwise. Strike Three! Don't know about you, but we have some hang-ups related to this heavy stuff. Sometimes we have to remind ourselves to get a grip.

> You're never quite good enough in Catholic school, are you?
>
> Pat P., VP of HRD
> Fortune 100 company

Mindset Challenge

Okay. Let's review these beliefs about original sin. Are you *really* tarnished or bad? Are you *really* unworthy? As a direct descendent of Eve, do you *really* represent the loss of paradise for all? We don't think so!

So get over it. Develop a different perspective on original sin. Actually, the concept is very freeing. The real lesson is that no one is perfect. This doesn't translate into the message that everyone is bad and should be on their knees repenting. Yes, no one is perfect, and better yet, no one ever will be. Phew, what a relief! You can throw away the goal of perfection and replace it with the goal of getting better every day. How freeing and exciting to let go of any attempts to achieve something that is unattainable and not feel guilty because you didn't attain it. Freed from the frustration and anxiety of being imperfect, we can embrace the thrill of growth and improvement. Now that's a mighty powerful mindset.

Don't confuse excellence, which is achievable, with perfection, which is elusive.

Anonymous

Shoot for the moon. Even if you miss you'll end up in the stars.

Les Brown
The Courage to Live Your Dreams

And do you know what else? You have already proven your inner strength. Years ago you were able to accept your less-than-perfect self and you didn't use it as an excuse to stop trying. You kept on truckin' and you're here now reading this book because you are pushing yourself to even higher levels. Seems like a pretty good character trait for leaders who have to keep going even in the face of adversity and failure. We Catholic girls are pretty awesome after all!

Let's check out how well you did with this first mindset challenge.

Quiz

Freed from the bonds of seeking perfection, my first instinct is to:

1. Drop dead from exhaustion
2. Head for the fridge
3. Feel guilty that I didn't try hard enough
4. Quit exercising
5. Scrub the kitchen floor on bare knees while praying the rosary
6. Keep trying to do my best

[If you answered 2 and 4, you're human. But 6 is the ideal answer, of course. If you answered 5, call the Catholic Girls Hotline immediately.]

#2   Men rule...Women drool

Let's face it, as Catholic girls, at least those educated before Vatican II, you had two paths to choose as you grew up. You could be pure, like Mary, or you could be more *colorful*, like Mary Magdalene. The latter was a sure path to hell, although Mary Magdelene redeemed herself quite nicely when push came to shove. There weren't any shades of gray—just black and white, heaven and hell.

Since Eve was made from only one of Adam's ribs, we knew (or were quickly taught) that men were innately superior beings. God was a man, we weren't. We couldn't be priests, we could be nuns. We couldn't even be altar boys, we could only serve on the Junior Altar Society and help clean the church. And to add insult to injury, we had to make the chapel veil statement—or for those of us pre-Vatican II babies, the mantilla statement—every Sunday. It always puzzled us why the boys had to take off their hats whenever they entered church and we had to put ours on. And worse yet, if we forgot our chapel veil, the nuns seemed to think the next best thing was a tissue. Clean or dirty, it didn't matter as long as we didn't sully our good name by appearing with a bare head.

Despite the 30 years of women's liberation efforts, and all the efforts before, many still see women as hormone-driven beings, often illogical or irrational. If you disagree with someone or get angry, you must have PMS. If you are perceived as too intelligent, too eager or aggressive, you are clearly someone to be feared and avoided. On the other hand, if you're meek, you might inherit the kingdom of heaven, but that corner office with a view will never be yours.

You were taught when you were very young that you were "less" than men. You got the message you were less worthy, less intelligent, less, less, less. Now as an adult, you may find that you're receiving confirmation of this old belief.

Mindset Challenge

What's a poor girl to do? Let's go back to the challenge process. First, seek to understand your mindset. How much of this do you really believe? Lay it out on the table and challenge it. Are you sometimes treated as inferior because that is how you treat yourself? Deep down do you believe you are inferior?

How do female leaders deal with this? They handle it pretty much the same way good male leaders do. They avoid extreme behaviors based on personal biases and they do whatever is necessary to ensure the success of their coworkers and themselves. They've learned that leadership is not about focusing on the innate difference between men and women or proving who's better (we are)—it's about finding common goals. Successful leaders are confident and

> *Don't bother just to be better than your contemporaries or predecessors. Try to be better than yourself.*
> William Faulkner

secure with their identities and realize that what they do and how they do it is their true measure, not how they compare to men. Female leaders who went to Catholic grade school need to know deep down what it's like to evolve from believing you are inferior to believing in and cherishing yourself. Your personal experience should allow you to look inside those you lead for the pieces of gold.

By challenging these old beliefs about men and women, you'll learn to chuckle and forgive. Maybe some of the teachings themselves weren't so bad, but the interpretations and the use left a lot to be desired. The important thing is not to throw them out completely. They are a very important part of your belief system. You just don't have to swallow the interpretations hook, line, and sinker anymore. Don't be fooled. These are big issues to embrace. For example, you no longer have to genuflect in the presence of a supreme being (man). In fact, as a general rule, it's better to stay off your knees completely! Challenge these beliefs, and others, one at a time. Don't give up. We'll get there. If only we could move faster in these darned high heels!

#3 Heaven and hell...
Nothing beats a great pair of L'eggs®

This challenge is a little different. In this case we are just going to tweak the belief. Heaven and hell in the true sense represent reward and punishment. The notion is very simple. If you earn your way through the pearly gates, you will be rewarded with eternal happiness—being in the presence of God. If you have earned punishment, you will be damned to the fires and suffering of hell. Now, maybe you've never given much thought to this interpretation. Maybe it was so absolute it was just an undebatable given. But we always looked at heaven and hell as "there will be justice in the end." We thought of it that way because we have always needed to believe in justice and fairness. And even though it wasn't great believing you had to wait until the afterlife, it was still enough to allow us to accept a less than fair world, as Patricia Zander discovered:

> I will never forget the sales call from hell. I had to fly out to meet a sales rep and help her demonstrate our medical equipment. Everything went wrong that could go wrong. The hospital biomedical person was not happy that we were descending upon his domain. He had blocked the equipment from being delivered to the lab where we were supposed to hook it up. So we (in our finest high heels) had to go get it from the opposite end of the hospital and push it all the way over to the lab. We had to go down to the shipping dock and pick up all our boxes. Then, he didn't have any of the cables we needed to connect it to the existing lab equipment, and on and on and on.
>
> There were two wonderful lab technicians (women) and he treated them as if they were an annoyance. Our troubles grew. He certainly was not going to help us. When his day was officially over he went home, but he was still on call. The four of us worked for hours and hours, trying to make the set-up work, including putting an urgent order in to a local surgical supply store for cables. We finally finished about 10:00 PM, and when we went to do the final

connections, we found we were missing one unique connector.

By this time we were exhausted and laughing at everything we did. Not wanting to give up when we were so close, we decided to call our not-so-friendly biomedical rep at home to see if he could find us that one connector. He begrudgingly agreed and said he would come in to look. As he entered the lab in his snowy white lab coat he was muttering under his breath how we couldn't get anything right. When he turned around we all saw his wife's pantyhose plastered to the back of his lab coat, permanently set with static cling as if the legs were dancing the *Highland Fling*. We thought we were going to die! None of us could speak or breathe as he strutted out of the lab into the hospital to find the connector.

He returned, unable to secure a connector, with the pantyhose firmly in place. We swallowed hard and thanked him. We never did get things up and running, and we didn't get the sale. But to this day, when I am in a difficult situation I think of those pantyhose and I am patient, for I know there will be justice in the end.

Patricia Zander, CEO/Owner
Oriel Incorporated

Mindset Challenge

If you have challenged the self-serving part of this belief, you may have mellowed, but only a little. We still hang on to the thought because it makes us more sensitive and aware of the good things that are fair or the little twists of fate that seem to set things right. In those situations we should quietly lower our heads and, with smiles on our faces, carefully look around the room to see if others are relishing the moment as we are. It can give you hope. Try it sometime.

#4 Self-sacrifice equals salvation

Do you know how many times you watched *The Song of Bernadette*? For our group it must have been dozens! That girl could scrub floors, and she never felt sorry for herself or whined. She was our idol!

> *To be successful, the first thing you have to do is fall in love with your work.*
>
> Sister Mary Laureth

Love your work. Fine. But never be a slave to it or marry it. The notion of self-sacrifice can get very twisted, sister. We learned self-sacrifice was good, and the best measure of self-sacrifice was the level of suffering you could endure. As a good Catholic girl in the workplace, you might be tempted to sign up for everything, work hideously long hours, and try to please everyone.

Remember, the more suffering, the better your performance, the stronger your commitment, and the purer your dedication. But while the nuns valued suffering, a healthy business world does not. Your organization needs leaders who will lead the organization with passion and energy, especially over the long haul. This requires a healthy level of sacrifice, commitment, dedication, discipline, and stamina—not burnout.

Mindset Challenge

Think about the last time that you made a sacrifice. Why did you
feel that you had to do it? What did you get out of it? Did anyone
benefit from the sacrifice part? With hindsight being 20/20,
would you do it again? Was it worth the pain? Was it all bad? The
fact that you embraced self-sacrifice when you were young is
actually a plus. Challenge yourself to think that the real lesson
shouldn't be about feeling pain and using pain to give your efforts
credibility. It's about doing much more than you ever thought
you were capable of. You're able to do what it takes to get results
in a variety of situations, including those that are uncomfortable.

Controlled self-sacrifice allows you to focus on a goal, a project, a
deadline, and give your all to getting it done. Sometimes you
should put yourself and your needs second, and put the needs of
others and the organization first. This is an incredibly valuable
part of your character and a must for a leader. But don't abuse it.
You can't and shouldn't totally disregard your "self." Learn to
keep things in balance. In the long run if you give, give, give, you
won't be able to help others or the organization. You'll burn out
and become resentful, comparing yourself to others and their
efforts. Too much sacrifice makes Jill a dull leader.

Love your work, but first love yourself. Do yourself a favor and
make yourself one of your pet causes. Hard work is fine, but don't
give 'til it hurts. Give 'til it's time to give back…to yourself.
Here's your new mantra, sweet Catholic girl: "The value of my

efforts is not determined by the amount of suffering. It's okay to nurture myself. I'm worthy." Patricia Zander shares another step in her leadership journey with us:

> We were opening a new sales and marketing center. It was beautiful: marble floors, carpeted walls, special track lighting, the works. The crown jewel of the center was the exhibit area where we would showcase our products. I was a proud product manager and I could see my products glimmering in the limelight.
>
> The unveiling of the center was to be part of the opening ceremony of our yearly stockholders meeting. Unfortunately, the center was still under construction the day before. I had all of my gear (pounds and pounds of computer-based medical equipment) to move in and set up. Late in the afternoon I went to conquer my area. I was a professional woman, up for any challenge, so I maintained my stately appearance and wore my high heels and dress.
>
> I hauled, carried, and set up the equipment as the plasterers worked on stilts over my head. Little flakes of plaster landed in my coifed hair, my brow developed unsightly sweat which attracted plaster dust like a magnet, and my feet, oh my God, my feet. But I knew deep down inside that I had arrived. I was doing all of this, and doing it in high heels. It was exhilarating! I couldn't wait for the CEO to come by and see. Well, he did. He suggested that I order myself a pizza or something, because it looked like a long night. And, oh yes, did I notice my arrangement of electrical cords was a little messy?
>
> Patricia Zander, CEO/Owner
> Oriel Incorporated

Mindset Challenge

Does this example challenge your beliefs about self-sacrifice? You
know what Patricia says she regrets? She regrets she didn't go
home first and change her shoes! She swears she would today.

#5 Thou shalt not go beyond the communion rail

Boundaries, boundaries, boundaries. There were so many
boundaries for Catholic girls it was amazing we ever made it onto
the schoolyard. As females, we weren't allowed past the
communion rail or into the sacristy, and we couldn't go near the
nuns' quarters without facing death. We knew where we were
welcome.

When we were planning this book we gathered together a group
of Catholic grade school graduates to share stories. Angela Prestil
told this story from her grade school years:

> A non-Catholic friend of mine wanted to see the
> inside of the church. So one day we slipped in when
> the church was empty. My friend marched right up
> the aisle to the front of the church. She climbed over
> the communion rail and strolled over to the
> tabernacle. She then proceeded to remove the
> tabernacle key and put it in her pocket as a cool
> souvenir. I just about died and couldn't sleep for
> days. But I didn't dare rat on my friend. That Sunday
> at Mass I watched in horror as the priest
> approached the tabernacle. I held my breath until I
> almost passed out, fearing he'd turn, stare directly
> at me, and ask where the key was.
>
> Angela Prestil, Project Manager
> Oriel Incorporated

Every one of those Catholic grade school grads gasped as she told her tale. No one could believe something awful didn't befall both the thief and her accomplice for this terrible deed. We shrunk down in our chairs as if lightening was sure to strike after this astounding confession. One woman in our group couldn't even get to the key part. She was still stuck on the fact someone went beyond the communion rail!

Mindset Challenge

For years we struggled with the Catholic boundary limitations. By now, hopefully, we think very differently. Knowing the importance of boundaries and knowing your own boundaries provides you with invaluable information about your environment. Yes, inappropriate boundaries are limiting and demeaning. But learning to respect boundaries is a very valuable lesson; it teaches you to respect others and their space. Every day we watch or interact with people who don't know enough to respect boundaries, and we see how hampered and ineffective they are in relationships and teams. For example, people with inappropriate boundaries may:

- Come into your office space and treat it as if it was their own, going so far as to read your mail or go through your desk
- Display overtly aggressive behavior
- Open cards sent with flowers and share the message with the group

- Give feedback or argue at a personal level rather than a business level
- Lack respect for authority and others' roles
- Eavesdrop on your conversations

One CEO we interviewed remembers a particular assistant she had helping her. This woman would listen intently to all of the CEO's phone conversations. She was so blatant that she would only type when the CEO wasn't talking, pausing and remaining quiet whenever the CEO spoke. With trust and honesty being such imperatives to good leadership, it isn't difficult to figure out why someone with poor boundaries would not be on the fast track to the top of the organization. Even though it may have been at an extreme level, consider yourself very lucky to have been exposed to boundaries.

Remember the most important exception: never allow anyone, especially yourself, to put boundaries on your imagination. You might be physically or in some other way restricted in what you can do or where you can go, but never stop learning, dreaming, and creating.

#6 Mea culpa, mea culpa, mea maxima culpa

Remember these Latin words we said during the Mass as part of the confiteor? Through my fault, through my fault, through my most grievous fault. Yes, of course it's all your fault. You're always ready to confess that you're a lowly sinner and most definitely not

worthy of anything good (as if you didn't know). You probably even carry this attitude into the workplace with all your other old beliefs. Well, it's your turn to try this one out on your own.

Mindset Challenge

Don't underestimate the issue of whether you are worthy of being successful. How are you going to react when you are a successful leader and you and your people receive praise for jobs well done? This may sound like a ridiculous question, and to many it would be, but not to most grown-up Catholic girls. We are often very good at figuring out how we will deal with our failures. Dealing with the deep feelings of unworthiness is not a small task, and it affects all aspects of your life. You may still laugh at, wonder about, and challenge your sense of unworthiness, but now you have to concentrate on completely overcoming it. Consider one of Patricia Zander's struggles:

> As long as I can remember I have been torn between the taste of chocolate and elastic waistbands. I have joined and dropped out of countless weight loss programs, including one that had audio tapes as part of the program. I began walking through the cemetery by my house every day after work, listening to the tapes. You were supposed to repeat after the voice on the tape, "I deserve to be thin." Well, I just couldn't say those words. Even alone in the cemetery, where no one could hear my words, I could not say them out loud. It drove me crazy, so I used to plan ahead. I'd pick out a specific gravestone where I was going to stop and say those words. I was so proud that after three months I had worked up to an audible mumble.
>
> Patricia Zander, CEO/Owner
> Oriel Incorporated

#7 God's will...Where there's a will, there's a weigh

How do you explain it when something went really well and you were sure it wouldn't? When we were young, we knew the answer—God's will. It was always God's will. You weren't to question, rail, or brag. You were to accept it on faith and move on. Forget cause and effect, that wasn't part of our faith.

> Everything that happened in our house when we were growing up was God's will. If you didn't get picked for the softball team, it was God's will. If you didn't get a date, it was God's will. If you got a huge zit on the end of your nose hours before the dance, it was God's will. If God wanted it that way, hey, Thy Will Be Done.
>
> In my family, we now make fun of it and take it to the point of absurdity. If a pair of pants fit, it's God's will that we buy them. If we find a chair that matches the carpet, it's God's will that we take it home. If we happen to pull onto a street with an ice cream drive-through, it's God's will we get the fudge sundae with whipped cream and peanuts. We laugh about it, but still when something big happens, we look at each other knowingly and say, It's God's will. The sad thing is I think we still believe it.
>
> Franny VanNevel, Writer

Mindset Challenge

This is a hard one to challenge because it can be so comforting and so fun. But here we go. The bad thing about believing in God's will is that it takes everything out of your control. Now

why is that so bad? You stand around waiting for a "sign from God" or the CEO, instead of daring to make things happen. If you really believe it then why experiment? Why try out new behaviors? Why learn from experiences? If it's God's will, then what is the use of trying to improve? Don't fall into the trap of using God's will as a crutch. In the extreme, it can let people deny responsibility. It can even allow them to be apathetic and complacent while it gives them comfort in knowing God is in charge.

The notion of God's will must have started out as a trick. Some priest who got tired of coming up with different answers every time his first grade class asked "why" invented the concept of God's will. (Only he probably said it in Latin!) Face it, even God doesn't completely accept the notion. If God did, then Adam and Eve would still be hanging out among the flora, and being a saint wouldn't be worth any points.

With God's will out of the picture, you are free to focus on cause and effect. This is a very important thing for a leader to do. But don't be too hard on yourself. Sometimes it just feels right to believe in fate, and yes, God's will.

> *I have my faults, but changing my tune is not one of them.*
>
> Samuel Beckett
> Nobel Prize-winning author and playwright

#8 This should be easy...Same stuff, different day

We are going to leave grade school and come back to current day to challenge your thoughts about what's necessary for you to succeed in the workplace. If you're new to the leadership role, and especially if you came up through the ranks of an internally competitive organization, you are in for quite a mind shift.

People are funny. When they learn to behave in a way that brings success they tend to use it over and over and over again, even if the environment or the task at hand has changed significantly. And how confusing when they get unexpected results. If you have been personally successful or promoted because you were the shining star, then it's time to stop and smell the coffee. Being an effective leader is not about being the brightest star in the night sky, it's about making sure all the stars shine. When we asked

Pat P. to give us an example of how she leads, she explained:

> I listen to people very carefully and I try to hear how their view is similar to my view and then I build on that. So it's leadership by listening. I have a sense of where I want to go and I tell them this: we're in California and you know you want to go to New York. We could take any number of roads, and the road we're going to take is dependent on what they want to do, how they want to handle it—do they want to go through mountains, through deserts? What is it that they would enjoy doing? And I try and describe what it's going to be like when we finally hit New York City, but I try and take us both through an experience that will get us there. I just take a lot of different roads to lead us to the same destination.

> Pat P., VP of HRD
> Fortune 100 company

Mindset Challenge

What do you believe is necessary for you to ensure your success as a leader? Reflect on a time that you were most appreciated and rewarded by the organization. Now push your memory of the situation. Why were you rewarded? Did you stand out in the crowd as someone really special? Were you the smartest and made sure everyone knew it? Did you compete against your colleagues and win (and they didn't)? Or did you lead a team to a successful completion?

Go back to Chapter 2 and review the common characteristics of leaders. Do these sound like things you were rewarded for in the past? If so, you are miles ahead. If not, think about the mind shift that you will need to make.

Genuflection

Go through the list of beliefs and adages in the table below. Think about what each of them meant to you as a young Catholic girl. Now look at your life and work today. Are those old beliefs still worthwhile? How? Can you take some pieces of your old beliefs and make them work for you today? What pieces do you need to leave behind in order to be successful today? Feel free to add a few of your own beliefs to this list.

When you're working through this exercise, remember not to throw the baby out with the holy water. Standing out, being competitive, being on the ball and knowing your stuff are all very important. You just have to know how to use these skills.

Belief or Adage	What did it mean to you as a Catholic girl?	Convert the meaning to make it useful in the workplace
God doesn't give you more than you can handle		
Suffering makes you grow		
Confess your sins		
God will strike you dead for your sins		
Divine intervention		
Don't hide your light under a bushel basket		
Add your own		
Add your own		

Benediction

The ability to challenge and modify your mindset is a very powerful skill. It is also very personal. If you are able to learn to reinterpret, leverage, and then cherish your early learnings and experiences, you will experience relief, forgiveness, and peace. As a leader you will often be alone, depending only on your inner self for strength, courage, and your own forgiveness. If that inner self is still bound by the beliefs of unworthiness, inferiority, and fear of your own light, you will be caught in an endless struggle. But if you have learned to master your attitude, to believe in and cherish yourself, your shine will light the way for others. Remember, how you approach tomorrow is up to you.

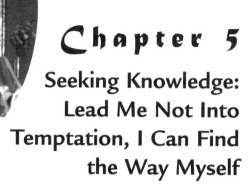

Chapter 5

Seeking Knowledge: Lead Me Not Into Temptation, I Can Find the Way Myself

• • • • •

*N*ow that you've learned to challenge and readjust your mindset, you're ready to make changes. In order to better understand how to improve your leadership abilities, you will first need to learn about yourself.

Back in Catholic school we spent hours and hours learning the Baltimore Catechism. What is grace? What is a sacrament? We studied in order to memorize. We memorized in order to obey. We obeyed in case we died. Let's not kid ourselves. The entire object of this was to get to heaven. If they were kind enough to canonize us after we died, we'd gladly add Saint to our name. At work, instead of fantasizing about getting into heaven, we've got our eyes on leading, the noblest of causes, or the corner office with Executive Suite on the door.

You don't lead by hitting people on the head— that's assault, not leadership.
    Dwight D. Eisenhower

In Catholic school we learned the rules and rituals. It was all gospel, hold the grain of salt. We nurtured our dream. We fantasized about the saints, our Guardian Angels, and we wondered what heaven was really like. The good Sisters would lead us in prayer and down the straight and narrow. If we weren't ready to learn, the Sisters were glad to pound it into us.

Seeking knowledge was never an issue in Catholic grade school. Those nuns kept the information coming so fast we didn't have time to blink, much less slouch. And just to make sure the nuns were doing their jobs, Father would pop in every once in awhile to test us on the Baltimore Catechism or last Sunday's sermon. He had to make sure Sister was steering us in the right direction— straight toward the seminary or convent.

Today's leaders don't have the luxury to learn passively. We have to seek out information and constantly expand our knowledge. And we must incorporate this constant learning into every facet of our daily work. There really is no rest for the wicked. Sorry, a little original sin flashback.

When you are seeking knowledge, imagine yourself as an explorer. As shown in Chapter 3, the opportunities to gain knowledge are endless. Sometimes you even pray they will stop presenting themselves. In this chapter we are going to focus on seeking knowledge of the world around you and the world inside you.

Put one foot in front of the other...

How do you learn the basics? When you are in a new organization, a new team, or a new role, where do you start? When we were young it was simple. We didn't "do" the Bible. We were passionately devoted to memorizing every single line of the Baltimore Catechism instead. That book defined our entire belief system and gave us a blueprint for our lives. We all could have been members of the "All-One-Mold Catholic Girls Club."

But being like everybody else in the workplace isn't enough— you're in a whole new world. This is the workplace, and there's a lot to learn about the leadership role. There's a new vocabulary, a dress code, corporate etiquette, changed relationships, and behaviors required of you. You must immediately learn enough to begin feeling comfortable, stay out of trouble, and present your authority as a leader. And if you're really lucky, you may actually impress those who are expecting to be impressed. As in Catholic grade school, you look to the rituals and rules, both explicit and hidden.

> *I'm going to ride the fence awhile until I find where the gates are.*
>
> Eva Bowring
> U.S. Senator

Little rituals, big messages

Rituals direct behavior. They are the prescribed activities played out in situations such as when a new employee is hired, when someone is promoted, or when someone has a major milestone anniversary with the company. Rituals are rich with information. They are like living paintings, allowing us an intimate look deep inside the organization. When we were young, we were involved in many rituals, including:

The Lure of Latin. For the more senior graduates of Catholic grade school, all the prayers and most of the songs were in Latin. Although we couldn't understand the meaning of the words, their emotions came through easily. The fact that we didn't understand the words only increased the mystery of the religion. It was as old and as sacred as Ancient Rome, and we were simply part of the continuum. Latin kept us firm in our faith and we found comfort in the rhythms of a language we could mimic and feel, but couldn't comprehend.

The Stations of the Cross. This ritual, played out every Friday during Lent, traced the final steps of Christ's life on earth as he made the journey to die for our sins. We were simultaneously heartened and humbled by the little side stories of faith and courage—Veronica wiping the face of Jesus, Simon helping Jesus carry the cross—that instilled in us the honor and responsibility of standing up for our faith in the face of adversity.

Scapulars, Medals, and Ashes. These were outward symbols of our internal faith and belief system. In our early years, these signified being a "chosen one." We belonged to the true religion and we would be saved.

Rituals in the workplace can be very powerful and often tell an important story about a company's history and culture. For example:

- The Operations Department at one company has a big party at the beginning of each month to celebrate all of the birthdays and anniversaries in that month. This builds a sense of camaraderie within the department, as well as giving the employees a chance to have some social interaction at work.

- Every new employee at one energy consulting firm is subjected to an intense orientation with the office manager which includes a two hour tour of the kitchen. The kitchen at this particular company is nothing special, but the two-hour tour emphasizes the importance of a clean and orderly environment to everyone in the company. If an employee leaves a dirty dish in the sink, they are chastised with comments such as "You must not have had your kitchen tour yet," and "I guess we'll have to have Chris give you another kitchen tour."

- At a major financial services corporation, annual meetings are punctuated by the speakers appearing in rank order, from the lowest ranking company official to the highest. Higher ranking officers do not even appear at the meeting until they are scheduled to speak, creating a fervor and excitement rivaled only by a personal appearance by Madonna. (The singer, not the saint.)

Pick out some of the rituals in place at your company and find out where they came from, how they started. Find out how the organization keeps them alive. Find out what the majority of people think of the rituals. You will learn a lot about the environment around you. And remember, you can create your own workplace rituals. They will become an important statement of your beliefs and leadership style.

Forgive me, Father, for I have sinned.
It's been 27 years since my last confession.

Rules are truly significant for the new leader. You are not only supposed to follow rules, you are now required to carry the torch for the rules, be the champion of the rules, and sometimes be the police officer of the rules. But when you are immersed in the rules and just trying to get through the day, you aren't focusing on your own leadership role. This can be a very difficult phase. You're caught between performing, toeing the line, helping others, getting results, and actively developing your own style of leading.

Learning the rules is critical. Remember the boundaries? You need to quickly understand the workplace parameters and how they impact your behavior. You will find that all rules are not created equal, and some are best dropped off at the nearest cemetery. (We will address this issue in Chapter 8. For now, let's focus on the value of gaining knowledge through understanding the rules.)

Obviously, you need to learn the rules if you are going to follow them. This is one of the first things a leader must do. Learning the rules also gives you invaluable insight about the world around you. Dig deep and find out why the rule is needed. Explore and find out who follows and who ignores the rule and why. Discover the various interpretations of the rule. Then step back and look at the overall number of rules. This will tell you a lot about previous and possibly current leadership styles.

Underneath her wimple she has curlers in her hair

Observe others and learn from them. Everyone has something to offer, whether positive or negative. During the meetings we held when we wrote this book, Patricia Zander gave us her twist:

> Whenever I was in a pinch, I always thought about leaders I admired and tried to imagine what they might do in my situation. What would they think? What would they say? If I was really in over my head, I pretended I was one of them and played the role to a tee. In fact, I got so good at it that I had different role models for different business situations. I bought clothes that were similar to what each of these role models would wear so I could perfectly coordinate the situation, the role model, and my clothes. And when I walked in the meeting room I was ready, calm, centered, and confident. Words would come out of my mouth that even I couldn't believe I had the confidence to say. I must admit, in my out-of-body state I was brilliant.
>
> I'll never forget the first time I became aware that I was role-playing. Many years ago, I was the product manager for a team that was developing a new medical device that required a type of highly specific plastic produced by only one manufacturer. We had a very unique opportunity and short window of time to bring in a large amount of new business if I could successfully develop this device. And our team was expected to seize this opportunity. We worked, we designed, we tested, we built prototypes, we tested, and tested some more. To our great surprise, we couldn't get any more plastic. Even though we had been promised the plastic, the manufacturer had changed their production schedule. This would delay our project and the window was shutting.
>
> So I called a meeting. As product manager it was my job to bring this issue to a "satisfactory" conclusion. We were all there (manufacturing, engineering,

service, inventory management, sales, accounting), and the plastic manufacturer brought all of their top-gun sales managers. I was sufficiently intimidated! But I also knew that I had to perform. I had to help bring about an acceptable solution.

I didn't know what to do. Sister Mary Josephina hadn't taught me to stand up to the priests and convince them that girls should get to be altar boys. But wait, maybe this wasn't so bad. I could just be someone else. I could imitate my corporate patron saint! I picked a CEO I admired and I decided to pretend I was him. (Yes, him. Hey, man or woman, I didn't care.) I knew just what he'd do. So I sat very calmly through all the talk, the posturing, the excuses. Then I very calmly said, "I appreciate your situation, but we have a schedule and your original commitment and we are going to figure out how we are going to meet both of these." In the end we got our plastic.

When it was over I took my shaking self back to my cubicle where I genuflected, made the Sign of the Cross, and looked up to heaven.

Patricia Zander, CEO/Owner
Oriel Incorporated

Patricia still uses imitation today because it is a natural way for her to learn to lead. In addition, the opportunities are certainly endless. But Patricia works hard at not misusing it. She realized that in those early years not only did she not have confidence in her own character and abilities, she had no clue what they were or even that they were important. So, when in need, she borrowed someone else's. It worked in the situation that day, but in order for her to be consistent and successful, to become an authentic leader, she needed to wear her own clothes and role-play herself.

The business: reading between the lines

We are not going to spend much time on methods for seeking knowledge about your business and markets. Depending on your role in the organization, you have access to information through many different channels. The important thing is to seek out the information. And don't take everything at face value. Talk to your customers, both internal and external. Listen and see for yourself. Feel the excitement and the emotion they are experiencing. You will need to be steeped in the business later on when we integrate all this information and knowledge and define desired behaviors.

Your character: the creature from the Black Lagoon

In Catholic grade school we learned that concentrating on ourselves and trying to be an individual wasn't important. It was, in fact, selfish and bad. According to the nuns, concentrating too hard on your "self" or your "needs" only led to trouble. (Do you think they learned this from experience?) Did you ever stare at your face in the mirror until all your features melded into some monstrous blob? That was the outcome for your soul if you worried too much about your "self." And, believe us, monstrous blobs did not make it into heaven.

We were taught that we were merely empty vessels, ready to be filled with the glory of God. Our job was to make sure the vessel was clean and as shiny as could be and that our goodness came not from ourselves but rather from God within the vessel. The

individual self was not to be known or nurtured, it was something to fear, ignore, or wrestle into subservience. This may be good advice for some, but it's very bad advice for a leader.

In order for leaders to behave consistently and with passion, they must continuously increase their understanding of how their character and personality affects their behavior and, in turn, the behavior of others. Through continuous learning and development, leaders make the necessary internal refinements, and then translate them into action. True leaders apply this process with vision, focus, and determination. Pat P. tells us one method she uses to help her own learning and growth:

> I get a lot of feedback from the people that I work with. The big question I ask when somebody who I work with leaves is what advice do you have for me? I get such great insight with that question.
>
> Pat P., VP of HRD
> Fortune 100 company

...And throw away the key

Unlike what we were supposed to believe in Catholic grade school, hardwired characteristics can profoundly affect our perception of the world and our behavior. Maybe that is why we were discouraged to know ourselves. Something as powerful as knowing who we were and how unique we were was best left locked away, and as feared as Pandora's box.

Opening Pandora's box, we find innate characteristics and personality traits that have a genetic base. Think of these characteristics as an extension of the nature-nurture concept; they represent the nature. Or think of them as the body type with which you were born, the way you walk, or the (natural) color of your hair. You are born with these traits that ultimately form the starting point of how you look, think, feel, and react to most things that you experience. And it is up to you whether they will represent the starting point or both the starting and the ending point.

No matter how much you grow and change, these hardwired characteristics will be with you for the rest of your life. But we don't have to think of them as reactions, thoughts, or emotions that we have to overcome. They are also not absolute determinants of how we can and will act. You are able to keep the negative in check and build on the positive. View these characteristics as the starting point for who you want to be and how you want to behave. By learning about these characteristics, you'll begin to understand why you think the way you do, why you react to intense situations as you do, how you make decisions, which situations will be the most comfortable for you, which situations will be the most difficult, and on and on.

A leader uses her innate, hardwired characteristics as a starting point, but continues to develop new behaviors and modify old behaviors so she isn't tied into some predetermined and unchanging state.

That was a close one!

In order to identify your hardwired characteristics, think about some examples. Think of the easiest way for you to learn a new computer program or the most comfortable way for you to learn how to develop a good golf swing, tennis swing, or mop swing. Remember, there is no right or wrong. Do you:

❑ Prefer to start out with detailed written instructions?

❑ Want to look at diagrams or pictures first?

❑ Want to have someone show you?

❑ Prefer a self-trial-and-error process?

Whichever method you most consistently use is typically a hardwired preference for the way you learn new things.

Think about examples of your reactions when you experience something that is very stimulating, such as narrowly missing a car crash, being offered the job you've always wanted, or being told your department was the best performing one in the company. Would you:

❑ Let out a shriek of joy (or despair)?

❑ Pleasantly smile (or frown) yet experience a charged reaction inside of you?

❑ Delay a reaction until you can think about it?

Think about when you are engaged in conversation. Identify what you use as the primary source of information from the other person and what you most respond to. Is it:

- ❑ The words that are being spoken by the other person
- ❑ The other person's tone of voice
- ❑ The other person's body language

Do you make decisions based on:

- ❑ Data and facts
- ❑ Intuition
- ❑ Feeling

And finally, think about when someone does something to you that you don't like. Do you respond with:

- ❑ Anger
- ❑ Hurt
- ❑ Thought (keep it all inside)
- ❑ Indifference (minimize the importance of it)

This book does not lend itself to providing you with an in-depth forum to learn about your own decision-making style, your character, or your hardwired characteristics, but don't let that stop you. Seek out other sources. (Recommended resources are listed in the References.) The value of understanding your hardwired characteristics is much more than a "find yourself" experience.

Knowing yourself is vital for your development as a leader. By understanding these characteristics and others, you will be better able to predict your own behavior, especially in intense situations.

Genuflection

Pull out the photo album in your memory. Open up the album and find the snapshots in your mind that depict the following:

You working very hard to do well.

- Why did you want to do well?

- How did it feel when you were working on this goal?

- What did it feel like when you were done?

People challenging you to be better or work harder.

- Who challenged you the most?

- How did their challenging affect you?

- Did you ever forgive them?

- Did you ever thank them?

You fell short or did not perform well.

- Did you survive it?

- How did you feel at the time?

- What affect did it have on you?

People who seemed to help bring out the best in you.

- Who were those people and how did they bring out your best qualities?

- What were the similarities between those people, if any?

Benediction

It is awesome to realize that the opportunity to learn from others, and about ourselves, is a gift that we can keep receiving over and over.

Chapter 6

Using the Process:
Becoming A
Smarter Martyr

• • • • •

magine it's Christmas. You're in fourth grade and
the school play is *The Birth of Christ*. The set is the
barn and the manger. There is a hush over the
crowd. The parents are lined up in those metal chairs, watching
and waiting for the big entrance. As you quietly wait behind the
curtain, you realize that every year you have dreamed of being
Mary, the Virgin Mother, to be selected to sit so serenely in her
humble dress made of sheets. Instead, you are one of the
shepherds. Your heart is heavy. But now it's your big moment. It's
time to go on. Your attention snaps back to the school play. You
adjust the rope on your headpiece and prepare yourself. You grasp
your staff and think of how important the shepherds actually
were, and you stand a little straighter. You are proud to represent
one of the keepers of God's flock. (Hey, it's better than being one
of the sheep!) When you walk out on the stage you project a sense

of wisdom, serenity, and confidence. You gaze compassionately into the eyes of the baby Jesus. You are your own unique shepherd, different than all the rest. And even though you don't say a word, everyone in the audience knows it.

The shepherd in you will come through gloriously because at the critical moment your inner character, your emotion, and the teachings of the parables will come together to create an image of what you want to be. Automatically, you will translate the image into actions, and you will act out your role.

Do you smell something burning?

In Catholic grade school we dreamed of being saints and martyrs. It wasn't something we did overtly. (Creative Behavior Day was not on the list of observed Holy Days of Obligation.) But it is something we did constantly in our thoughts and play. We imagined how we would act if we were burned at the stake. Would you cry and give in, or would you stand tall and silent? If you had been with Jesus in the Garden of Gethsemene, would you have been like Judas or would you have sprung to Jesus' side and cut off the other ear? We dreamed of a dramatic situation and we imagined what we would do, down to the finest detail. And our imagining was filled with our own sense of how we would do it even better when it was our turn.

Translating knowledge into behavior is where everything starts to come together for you as a leader. This is where deep change is experienced and where generic leadership is transformed into your own unique style. Here you have the opportunity for creativity and experiencing the sense of coming home. Eventually you will be acting both as a leader and as yourself at the same time. You will come back to this process over and over again because this is how you change.

In an instant our little shepherd had an image of who she wanted to be and automatically turned her vision into reality. She was functioning at the innate character level and reacting with behaviors that were habitual. A leader moves beyond the innate, adding new, desired behaviors to her core.

> *If you can dream it, you can do it.*
>
> Walt Disney

In this phase you are an artist. You mold yourself into the image of the kind of leader you want to be by bringing together your desire to change, your beliefs and values, and your knowledge. And this image is made real by your actions.

Did we mention process? Now don't complain about why translating knowledge into behavior has to be a process. It really doesn't complicate things; it's supposed to make things better. Really.

> **Process:** *The grouping, in sequence, of all the tasks directed at accomplishing one particular outcome.*

For some, process spells relief, for others, fear. Truth is, you use processes all the time. The sequence of steps you go through to take a shower, get dressed, put on pantyhose, take out the trash, and to get your kids to take out the trash are all different processes.

The only commandment

In order to systematically improve any activity it must be addressed as a process. If you want to systematically improve your leadership abilities through experience and learning, then you must use a process.

When you lay out individual steps as a process you will gain valuable insight as you see tasks as a series of related events. This might provide an unexpected challenge because even though all day, every day, everyone follows processes, most people don't think in these terms. Instead, they see the steps as isolated events.

By creating a process for translating knowledge into behavior we are able to define the starting and ending points, as well as the in-between steps required to generate the desired results. This provides a way to measure and refine your efforts so you can control and improve the results.

> **Our First Commandment:** *You can't improve the results unless you improve the process by which you generate them.*

The goal is to learn to define specific, effective leadership behaviors that are true to your identity. (Ignore any feelings of low self-confidence. They are forbidden in this chapter.) Some of these behaviors will be modifications of the old and some will be completely new.

We will call this process the Translation Process (translating knowledge into behaviors). We will be using a simple but powerful tool, the SIPOC model, to help us.

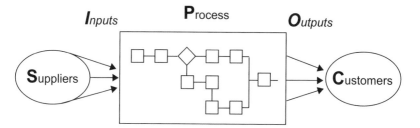

SIPOC is a way of defining the key elements of any process. In this case we are applying it to the process of defining desired behaviors. SIPOC can easily be translated into common elements for many leaders.

S = Suppliers

Suppliers are people or places (sources) where you can get information about yourself and the environment. Your Suppliers may be:

- You
- Your assistant
- A mentor
- Your boss
- Those you supervise
- Books

- Trainers
- Coaches
- Friends
- Reports
- Your job description
- Personal assessment results

I = Inputs

Inputs consist of relevant information about yourself and the environment. This is the type of internal and external information discussed in Chapter 5. For example:

- Results from leadership style assessments
- Feedback
- Your own insights
- Corporate directives
- Organizational policies
- Description of job duties

P = Process

Process is the sequence of steps you go through to turn the Inputs into Outputs. For the Translation Process it's how you take what you know and come up with your best idea for a desired behavior.

O = Outputs

An Output is the desired behavior.

C = Customers

Customers are the recipients of your service, behavior, or actions. Your Customers may be:

- You
- Those you lead
- Vendors
- Your banker
- Your boss
- Stockholders
- Board of directors
- The purchasing customer

Teri's and Anne's excellent adventure

The Translation Process is very dynamic. We will begin by following a straightforward path. In reality you will weave in and out and back and forth among the elements. To illustrate how the process works, we have enlisted two Catholic grade school graduates, Theresa Catherine and Anne Marie, to help us. They are very different from each other, each having her own leadership style. Both are highly effective and well respected. We are going to put them in the same business scenario, and, for our purposes, we will expect the same **desired outcome.**

Teri's and Anne's initial approach to the Translation Process will be different because each woman has her own style of thinking about a task. Remember how important knowing about your style is? Here is another instance where it comes into play. You'll see that both Teri and Anne get to the end of the process with the same desired outcome, but they certainly take different paths to get there. Your style may be different than either of these, so don't blindly copy their examples. Make sure you outline your own specific behaviors. At the end of the chapter we will show you a completed SIPOC diagram for Teri and for Anne to show you how two people completed the Translation Process. Remember, your process will be very different.

We'll warn you that this is going to feel cumbersome, strange, and formal at first. But it's like riding a bike. The more you do it the more it becomes second nature. Before you know it, you'll be sailing through the steps unconsciously. And don't forget Our

First Commandment: *You can't improve the results unless you improve the process by which you generate them.* That directly translates into "You must also *follow* the process." Discipline! Discipline!

So let's begin. Allow us to introduce you to Theresa (Teri) Catherine. Teri's nickname is "Jane-of-All-Trades." Someone working with Teri would describe her as being:

- A "typical manager"
- Driven by outcome: accountability, productivity, and results
- Hands on
- Blunt
- Surprised when people view things differently
- Comfortable learning through hearty debate

Some things Teri has trouble with:

- Being tactful
- Being committed to a process
- Being clear about differences between asking and debating

Now we'll introduce you to Anne Marie. Anne's motto is "Just Go and Do It." Someone working with Anne would describe her as:

- Frequently misunderstood and often underestimated
- Effective at most things but often seen as unorthodox
- Keeping a low profile
- Thinking things through before verbalizing them
- Having strong analytical skills
- Common-sense driven

- Impatient, with highly emotional reactions
- Theorizing without data
- Wanting to *do* more than *plan*

Some things Anne has trouble with:

- Having an agenda and stating it
- Telling people what she wants or doesn't want from them
- Describing out loud how she has used people's input
- Acknowledging she appears less invested than she really is
- Listening, listening, listening

The Translation Process

Now that we know our two players, we can get on with the business at hand. You'll have a chance to spy on Teri's and Anne's thoughts as we walk through the process. We will start the "adventure" by giving Teri and Anne a **desired outcome.** For yourself, identify what you would like to see happen as a result of becoming a better leader. You will be working through the Translation Process to identify what you have to do in actions, attitude, and approach in order to achieve your desired outcome. Describe it as an outcome, a goal, or as a result. Be very specific. It is often easiest to define an outcome relative to a problem being solved. But don't limit yourself. Think about issues and interactions that are not problem-related, and anticipate your desired outcome.

Teri: What do I want to have happen? I want people I work with to take me seriously when I ask for input. And to improve my review results. I could get their ideas quicker and we could speed up our work processes. Maybe I should talk with each one of them? Okay. It said not to look for solutions yet.

Anne: I don't want to do this. I already know what the outcomes will be. And if I don't, I'll figure it out as I go. This is just another "planning exercise" that looks good on paper but won't work. I bought this leadership book for a reason, though, so I guess I should at least try this. I guess I'd better give it five minutes. There I go, slipping back into my Catholic guilt mode. Interactions and outcomes, hmmm. I guess my staff does tell me that I don't want their input when I really do. I guess I could try that.

So Teri and Anne are going to start off with the same challenge or **desired outcome**:

*That my coworkers and staff know I am
sincere in wanting their input*

In order to reach your goal, you have to know who will be affected and how you would like them to respond. Work on a small scale and focus on the desired results for those who will be directly affected by your actions—your **Customers** (C). We traditionally think of Customers as the people who pay for our product or service. Broaden that definition to include those who receive the benefits of your daily tasks, your conversations, or your actions. Begin by reviewing the list of potential Customers on page 80. Can you think of anyone in your work situation that parallels the roles listed? Are there other people who would be considered Customers of your actions? Because Teri and Anne are in the same business scenario, we'll give them the same Customers: coworkers and staff. But how they decided on these two groups was certainly unique for each of them:

Teri: Okay, let's see. What are we supposed to do? Come
          up with a list of who our Customers are. Their list
          says "Those you lead." I get a lot of feedback from
          my staff in my yearly reviews, even though I don't
          always like what they have to say. The other big
          group of people that I work with every day is my
          coworkers. In fact, I do more for them than my
          boss. So I guess those would be my two groups of
          Customers.

Anne: Here we go already! I knew there was a reason I
          didn't want to do this. I already know how it'll turn
          out. Define those who are affected by my actions?
          It's so simple. My staff certainly gets the benefit of
          my wisdom. And of course I want feedback from the
          other people in my department.

Teri and Anne have just completed the Customer element of the
SIPOC diagram as shown on pages 94 and 95. Now that Teri and
Anne know what they want to achieve and who their Customers
are, it's time for them to **define the Suppliers** (S) **and Inputs** (I)
elements of the SIPOC diagram. There are two ways to fill in
Suppliers and Inputs. Some people start with the Suppliers and
define what each has to offer. Others define the information they
need and then determine who has it and how to get it (Inputs). If
you begin by listing the Inputs you need, fill in the corresponding
Suppliers who can give you that information. Then review your
Suppliers. Have you left out a potential key source of information?
If so, what is it they have to offer as an Input?

Suppliers are the people who will provide Teri and Anne with
information about their current leadership styles that will help
them become better leaders. Think about the people or things

that give you feedback on a regular basis, both formally and informally. Push yourself to move beyond only verbal or written feedback. Who or what gives you direction on a daily basis? Does your job description drive your actions, or is it the grant you received last year? Refer back to the list on page 79 to get started, but remember to be very specific in naming who your Suppliers are. In many cases, your Customers may also be your Suppliers, but here you should list them individually by name.

Inputs include the type of information available to Teri and Anne from their Suppliers. Think about the ways you have received information about your job performance, your daily actions, or your conversations. You certainly get verbal feedback, and you may also have a formal, written review. Consider how you gathered information as a Catholic grade school girl. You didn't have to be hit by Sr. Mary Margaret's ruler to get the message that giggling during morning prayers was unacceptable. And how did you know that Sr. Jane was a pushover before you were in her class? You gathered Input through stories, rules, personal observation, and experience.

Teri and Anne both start by looking at some of their Customers as Suppliers, and then listing what each Supplier can give them as an Input:

Teri: Okay, let's see. I need to make a list of my Customers. I'll start with the easy ones, listing my coworkers and my direct reports. The input I get from Tim, Vickie, and Deb is really pretty similar to the input I get from Bill, Sue, and Rich. They all will be able to give me their comments on how they know whether I'm sincere or not when I ask for input. Oriel suggests listing a mentor. You know I never really did have a good mentor here at work, but the best I could come up with would be Chris, so I'll put Chris on the list. He gives me some really good advice on pitfalls that I don't always see.

I know another Supplier I could list—previous coworkers. They always gave me information even if I didn't want to hear it. You know I never really did get along that well with any of them, but the ones I got along with the best were Dave and Lisa. They could certainly tell me when they thought I was being sincere and when they thought I wasn't, and what made a difference to them. Okay, they also suggest listing friends, but the friends I have are mostly outside of work. They may not be important here, but I'll go ahead and put them down anyway. They should certainly be able to tell me when they think I'm being sincere.

Another source of information I should list is some of the stories I've heard about leaders around here who really showed sincerity. Those stories could probably teach me a lot, especially the one about the leader who couldn't get anyone to take him seriously. And I can't forget myself. That's at the top of the list, and I do have to do some thinking about why people don't think I'm sincere. Oh, I should go back and take a look at the reviews that I got last year to see what that says about me, too.

Anne: See, I try to go along and here I am already deep in this "planning" process that I hate. It's just going to add time to getting things done. But I've still got 4 minutes and 30 seconds left on the time I was willing to give to this. Define the Suppliers and gather Input? What does that mean? This must be the part where you get feedback. I already know what people are going to say. Well, Beth is pretty good at telling me stories with valid points, so I guess I'll put her down. I can also ask Ralph. I guess I'd consider him to be a mentor. He's been pretty decent about steering me through the politics here. I hate to say it, but I think this is going a little bit quicker than I thought!

I guess friends can be Suppliers, too. Even though Sally is just my neighbor, she really knows me. We don't really talk about work much, but I know she can tell when I'm being sincere. I put coworkers as one of my Customers, so I could list that. Jane is always really honest with me. And I also listed my staff as Customers, but I don't want to look desperate, so I won't start with them.

What else is on the list? Me? Like I could really find out anything I don't know already! What am I supposed to do, interview myself? And personal assessment results? Way too touchy-feely for me.

Time for a little review. Step back and imagine what achieving your desired outcome will mean. For Teri and Anne, what will it be like to have people know that they're sincere in wanting input, and then to actually get it? Many of us are ready with the contingency plan if things don't go as planned. Don't forget to anticipate what it will be like if things go well. This may lead you to gather more information, in which case you should update your Suppliers and Inputs.

Teri and Anne have just completed the S and I elements of the SIPOC model as shown on pages 94 and 95. Teri selected 11 people, including herself, as Suppliers, and she included a personal inventory she took. She also identified the type of information, or Inputs, each Supplier could give her. Anne, on the other hand, came up with four Suppliers and their corresponding Inputs. For both Teri and Anne, the people they listed as Suppliers interact with them in different ways and are able to provide them with feedback and Input on a variety of issues. When working through the Translation Process, it is important to make sure your Suppliers will give you a broad range of Input.

Once Teri and Anne have gathered the Input from their Suppliers, it's time to translate the Inputs they received into specific **desired behaviors,** or **Outputs** (O), and to figure out what **Process** (P) they will have to go through to make those desired behaviors everyday actions. We know that this part of the Translation Process isn't easy, so we have some hints to get you started:

- Integrate the internal and external knowledge you have gathered as Inputs.

- Compare this knowledge to the expectations that your Customers have. Stick to the list you've generated in your SIPOC diagram.

- Using this knowledge, identify the customer expectations you think you will meet and not meet without a behavioral change.

- Think up new behaviors, or pull from your existing repertoire of behaviors, those that seem likely to have a good chance of meeting the previously unmet expectations.

Make sure you describe the behaviors as specific actions, not as desired outcomes. For instance, "I will be honest" describes an outcome. "I will answer all questions truthfully and not answer questions for which I don't know the truth" describes a specific action. A simple test is to state an Output and then ask yourself "How will I do that?" If you have described actions, you will know how you will take action. If not, keep working.

Defining specific behaviors is an acquired skill and may be a new challenge for you. When you first go through this you will probably be defining what you think needs to be done (by the book, or imitation) versus being much more creative and exercising free will. This is similar to following the Baltimore Catechism, only with a little less direction. At first, the culture, the policies, and the directives you have been given will dictate much of how you behave. But as you try out your new behaviors and learn from them, you will begin to develop your own unique behaviors and approaches.

Teri: Okay, chart the Process. Let me see. Some of the information I get from coworkers is that they don't think I'm very sincere because my voice doesn't change much and I'm always talking about getting things done quicker. So I guess that's something I better work on.

Now for Chris, my mentor. When I talked to him, in true mentor form, all he did was ask me a lot of questions, like "Would I listen to myself?" and "Do I sound sincere to myself?" I don't know what he was getting at, but I think he was saying that I really don't come across with much enthusiasm or interest. He also implied I don't listen well.

The next area is previous coworkers. I talked to them and they said they always took the shortcut by trying to translate what I meant. After a while they got pretty good at it, but they did say it was pretty frustrating.

Let's go on to friends. My friends say that they've learned my language, but they said that it would be a lot easier if I could say what I meant. Also, some of them implied that I interrupt before they get done telling me their thoughts.

The next category is me. Boy, that's still confusing. I guess I'll have to come back to that later.

Okay, reviews are my last area to fill in. Let me get out these old inventories. Well, the inventories do say that I'm pretty blunt and I'm outcome-driven. I wonder what that means? I guess it means that I'm interested in getting to the results as quickly as I can. So speed is good, but I wonder if I lose people in the process?

Anne: Ralph told me that if I would at least give a quick summary of what I'm thinking, even if it's not my final thought, that might be helpful. He's probably right. Maybe if I started by saying, "This is not in final form yet, but I've been thinking. . .," that would help. I should also try to listen, or at least give the impression that I'm listening better than I have before. I know people say that to me all the time, including my kids. And I guess I could also tell people more specifically what I want from them. Jane told me that it might help to write out my thoughts beforehand. Beth suggested giving comments throughout a conversation instead of waiting until the very end so people don't feel as if I'm judging them. Egad! Look how I'm following along.

Teri and Anne made sure they asked their Suppliers for specific Input, which helped them identify how they needed to change their behaviors. They also worked through the Process they'll need to implement in order to achieve the Outputs that would help them reach their goals.

Determine what it will be like for you, personally, to act in the way you have defined. Check your Inputs, such as past experiences and data from your assessments and other sources. For example, you want people to feel comfortable challenging your ideas. What will it mean for you to behave in a way that will encourage them to come forward? Maybe if you're as nice as The Flying Nun, it will be easy for people to approach you; but now you come off as intimidating, making this much more difficult.

Remember, there are no right or wrong styles, but there definitely is a good fit and a poor fit, effective and not. Some behaviors will be easy for you, because they will simply be modifications of what you currently do well. Others will be challenging to define and more challenging to do. Actively seek Input. For example, if you want people to feel comfortable challenging you, ask those who have actually challenged you in the past if they felt comfortable doing so. Whether their answer is yes or no, ask them to describe what you did that made them feel that way.

You may find after this analysis that you will need to tweak your behaviors. Or, to increase your success, you may need to add some new behaviors that need to be in place before you can achieve your final goal. You may find it helpful to go back and change your Suppliers, Inputs, or Outputs at this point. Remember, Rome wasn't built in a day, so give yourself time to work through your new Processes to make sure you end up with positive results and achieve your desired outcome. Take some baby steps before you leap into a whole new way of operating. It'll be easier for you, as well as your Customers!

Teri: It looks like I have to do a better job of listening, at least that's what several people are telling me. I wonder what that would be like for me. It might feel like I'm wasting time. Or it might feel like I already know what people are going to say, so maybe I should just fill in the blanks for them. And changing my voice is going to feel pretty corny at first. But I guess what I'm realizing is that it does take away from people's belief that I'm interested in them. And if my long-term result is to get the input quicker, maybe I ought to listen better and take a little more time on the front end so I can get to the end result quicker.

Anne: Why do I have to change? I just need to have other people read my mind better. That's it! I'll give them the Psychic Hotline number. Then maybe they can get this stuff quicker. I know, I'm whining. Maybe there are some shortcuts here. I wish people did know that I really do want their reactions. This is going to be hell! Somebody better call a priest to give me the Last Rites.

Teri's and Anne's completed SIPOC diagrams are shown on pages 94 and 95. At this point they will take one last opportunity to review their diagrams to see if the defined behaviors fit who they are and what they now know about themselves and their organizations.

Teri's Diagram

Suppliers	Inputs	Process	Outputs	Customers
Coworkers: Tim, Vickie, Dave	Comments on whether they know I'm sincere or not and what made the difference	1. Let my coworkers and staff know I am trying to make positive changes	Listen better	Coworkers
Staff: Bill, Sue, Rich		2. Show interest when others talk by using active listening skills	Vary my voice	Staff
Mentor: Chris	Advice on pitfalls		Don't interrupt	
Previous coworkers: Dave & Lisa	Feedback on when they thought I was being sincere and when I wasn't	3. Think through what I'm going to say to make sure I cover all of the key points	Explain my thoughts	
Friends	Feedback on when I'm being sincere			
Organizational stories	Memories from myself and others	4. Take the time to fully explain the points I'm covering	Slow down	
Me	Information from previous experiences	5. Get feedback to make sure people do really know I'm being sincere		
	Image of myself being successful			
Personal assessment results	Written report from my assessment			

Anne's Diagram

Suppliers	Inputs	Process	Outputs	Customers
Coworkers: Jane	Honest information and feedback on my level of sincerity	1. Plan what to say—write out my thoughts ahead of time	Written out thoughts beforehand, including questions asking for reactions	Coworkers
Mentor: Ralph	Information on potential pitfalls and problems to consider; things to think about	2. Actively listen and interact—my silence may mean something different to others	Give comments periodically—don't wait until I've reached a final conclusion	Staff
Previous coworkers: Beth	Stories about similar situations	3. Respond honestly— showing emotion doesn't mean I'm out of control	Listen, listen, listen and don't run away from emotions	
Friends: Sally	Conversations about friends and some discussion around sincerity in general		Ask for reasons why people say things and what info they are using	

Fasten your seatbelt, it could be a bumpy ride

You're almost ready for take-off: **Do a final check**. Is the defined behavior really you? Is it what the organization needs? Don't ask whether you have ever done this before, or whether it will surprise people. Instead, ask yourself:

❑ Would this behavior be consistent with my values and principles?

❑ Would this behavior be consistent with the policies of the organization?

❑ Would this behavior be consistent with my thought process?

❑ Would this behavior be consistent with my respect and regard for others?

❑ Would this behavior be consistent with my passion?

❑ Will the organization benefit from it?

❑ Will my Customer see the value in it?

If you can answer yes, then you are ready to take your new behavior out for a test drive. If the answers are no, run through the Translation Process again. Push yourself as far as you can to make the behaviors, or Outputs, consistent with who you are and with what the organization needs from you.

• Force yourself through a pros and cons analysis.

• Remember to look at your new behavior from your Customer's point of view.

When you're ready to go, enlist the help of a coworker or mentor whom you trust will be honest with you. Have them watch you interacting with others and then share with you what you did, both when you had the desired effect and when you didn't.

Remember that being able to translate knowledge into behavior is a very difficult task. As with most things, it gets easier with experience. But it's worth the effort. The turning point comes when you begin to exhibit your own style and you achieve your desired results! And as you lead, this is where you will return often, to improve, refine, and hone, just like the master craftsperson you are becoming. Through this process you become the genuine article.

Limping down memory lane

Let's take a quick trip back to Catholic grade school. There were valuable lessons we learned from the saints. They were true to themselves and their beliefs. They held on to their uniqueness even in the face of adversity and crisis. After all, that's what made them saintly. Being true to yourself and your beliefs will help you become the best leader you can be, every day. By the way, the saints also died for the cause, so don't take this lesson or process too seriously. A colleague shares her story about her "saintly sister":

> When we went to mass as part of school—for First Friday, Holy Days of Obligation, or the Nuns-Didn't-Make-a-Lesson-Plan Day—we always sat with our class. First graders toward the front of the church, second graders behind them, and so on. And we always had mass before lunch so we could abide by the "fasting for an hour before communion" rule. We'd all be starving, it'd be hot in church, the place would be packed with kids in smelly tennis shoes, and we'd have to practice our Catholic calisthenics in perfect timing with all of

those around us. (Stand up! Sit down! Fight! Fight! Fight!)

One year on Ash Wednesday or St. Blaise day, or one of those days when you had to parade up to the front of the church for more than just communion, I remember being particularly hungry. My sister and I had been running late that morning, and a piece of dry toast was about as square as our meal got for breakfast. I was dying for that communion wafer— then I'd be filled with the Holy Spirit and would hunger no more. Or something like that. We had already made one trip through everyone in church for their ashes or candle blessing, which added a solid 15 minutes to the length of the mass.

I was in third grade, so our class was first in line for communion, thank God! I was just getting to the front of the line to get that delicious, dry, paper wafer in my mouth when I heard the telltale thud of someone fainting in the pews behind me. There were so many people standing up for communion I didn't even know until I got home that night that the thud I heard was the sound of my sister's head hitting the pew. Mom always said she was bucking for sainthood.

Angela Prestil, Project Manager
Oriel Incorporated

Genuflection

Well, girlfriend, this is the moment of truth. Actually it's more like the moment when truth collides head-on with how you think the world around you operates. You have all the right stuff. You have desire, you've made a mindset adjustment, you've learned about yourself and the business world, and you've integrated all the pieces. Now it's time to take your newly developed behaviors out into the work environment.

To prepare you for this experience, take some time to **fill out your own SIPOC diagram using one of the outcomes below that would be appropriate for displaying one of your new leadership characteristics.** Think through the scenario and evaluate how your innate character and core beliefs will influence your behavior. Set a goal for what you want the outcome to be. Decide what behaviors will be most effective. Remember, this isn't imitation or following a script. You should be focusing on exhibiting behaviors that fit the situation and that result from your unique leadership style.

My desired outcome is to:

- Operate from a basis of respect
- Model desired behaviors
- Be decisive
- Use humor appropriately
- Encourage others to take risks
- Show my vulnerability

Benediction

Developing and using new behaviors can be scary,
especially if you are still dealing with those self-confidence
issues. But even if you make mistakes, you will be
consistent and trustworthy. Remember that nobody
follows someone they don't trust, and everyone is drawn
to someone with courage.

Chapter 7

Feedback: Never Do Cartwheels in a Skirt

• • • • •

You are ready to receive the sacraments. You have done your homework, you know what you want to do, and you are ready to march down that aisle. Bow your head, make the sign of the cross, stand up straight, and step out of that pew into the work environment, armed with your new behaviors. You have planned and now is the time to act. You're on. Sometimes you will receive a standing ovation and sometimes you won't. You will have success and you will have disappointments.

The only people who fail are those who never try.
Ilka Chase
Actress

The truth will set you free

Changing your behavior is much like learning to walk, ride a bike, ski, or apply mascara. You can think about it, visualize it, and plan it, but in the end, you just gotta do it. Your goal is to make sure you ask someone you trust to give you honest feedback, especially in situations where you will be immersed in just trying to get through it. You know you'd want someone to tell you if your mascara was giving you raccoon eyes, right? So even if it's difficult, you have to be open and willing to receive feedback to be an effective leader. Nancy Buechel remembers a notable situation from her grade school days in which feedback was sorely lacking:

> If you did something right for the teacher you would get a bag of candy. I never got that bag of candy and I never really knew why. So that was probably the only thing that I remember failing at, and I was clueless.
>
> Nancy Buechel, Financial Aid Office Supervisor
> University of Wisconsin-Madison

In the previous chapter we talked about translating knowledge into behavior. We went through a thorough examination of whether or not the new behaviors were aligned with your customer's expectations, business objectives, and your own style. Now it's time to get out there and see what happens.

Think through how you will measure the success of your efforts. You might, for example, measure the number of responses to a memo. You might record how close a meeting began in relation to its scheduled start time, the ability to reach consensus, and the like. Or you could use a "grading system" with which you are familiar. By using a simple measurement you can begin to determine whether changes you make have the desired effect. Make sure you have a way to collect information about the actual results, preferably from several different vantage points. The verdicts may be very different.

CITIZENSHIP, CHARACTER. AND HEALTH

THE HABITS AND ATTITUDES LISTED BELOW ARE DESIRABLE TRAITS FOR GOOD LIVING. THE TEACHER HAS INDICATED THOSE WHICH HAVE STOOD OUT AS DISTINCTLY COMMENDABLE, AS WELL AS THOSE FOR WHOSE FURTHER DEVELOPMENT THE COOPERATION OF THE PARENTS IS DESIRED.

A—INDICATES TRAITS IN WHICH THE PUPIL IS OUTSTANDING
B—INDICATES TRAITS IN WHICH THE PUPIL IS SATISFACTORY
C—INDICATES TRAITS IN WHICH IMPROVEMENT IS NEEDED

(A CHECK (√) AFTER AN ENTRY INDICATES THAT IMPROVEMENT HAS BEEN SHOWN)

TRAITS	7 WEEKS	13 WEEKS	FIRST TERM	7 WEEKS	13 WEEKS	SECOND TERM
OBEDIENCE (CHEERFULLY OBEYS RULES AND REGULATIONS BOTH OF CHURCH AND SCHOOL; IS AT THE RIGHT PLACE AT THE RIGHT TIME READY FOR WORK; HAS WORK COMPLETED ON TIME.)	A	A	A	A	B	B
SELF-CONTROL (USUALLY THINKS BEFORE ACTING; RESTRAINS HASTY IMPULSES)	B	A	A	A	B	B
PERSEVERANCE (PUTS FORTH BEST EFFORT; KEEPS ON TRYING IN SPITE OF FAILURE)	A	A	A	A	A	A
COURAGE (ATTACKS DIFFICULTIES WITH CONFIDENCE; IS READY TO ACKNOWLEDGE MISTAKES AND TO MAKE AMENDS; DOES WHAT IS RIGHT REGARDLESS OF REMARKS OF COMPANIONS.)	A	A	A	A	A	A
COOPERATION (RESPECTS RIGHTS OF OTHERS; WILLINGLY JOINS OTHERS IN WORK AND PLAY; IS COURTEOUS AND CONSIDERATE TOWARD OTHERS)	A	A	A	A	A	A
ORDERLINESS (KEEPS DESK. BOOKS, AND OTHER MATERIAL IN GOOD ORDER, PREPARES AND ARRANGES WORK NEATLY)	A	A	A	A	A	A
HEALTH HABITS (KEEPS FACE, HANDS, NAILS, AND TEETH CLEAN; IS CLEAN IN HABITS OF DRESS; SITS, STANDS, AND WALKS CORRECTLY)	A	A	A	A	A	A

A cast of thousands...or at least 5

1. **Pick them.** So where do you begin if you're searching for good, honest feedback? First of all, you need to bite the bullet and pick three to five of your coworkers or direct reports with whom you interact on a regular basis. And don't just choose the people who like you. If you want honest opinions, you have to mix it up a little. Do you always get into a heated discussion with Millie from the mailroom? Then see if she'd be willing to give you some honest feedback. Is Patty from purchasing your best buddy? Then maybe you don't want to ask for her help with this—can she truly be objective? Hey, we told you back in the first chapter that there might be a little suffering here. Just remember that it's for your own good.

2. **Tell them they've been picked**. We've identified the observers who will give us feedback. Now what? Ask each person individually if they would be willing to provide you with specific, constructive feedback on a work situation of your choosing. It will work best if you can get two different angles or perceptions on the same situation. Is there a staff meeting where your observers could see you in action? Is there another situation that one observer would normally be present for that you could invite another to attend?

3. **Prepare them.** Once you've got the timing down, it's up to you to determine what you'd like to practice and get feedback on. If your observers are new to this feedback process, you

might want to brief them ahead of time. Tell them a little bit about what you've been working on so they know what to pay attention to when you're talking. Can you imagine going through all of this only to find out that your observers weren't listening at the critical moment or didn't seem to understand what you wanted from them? Then again, maybe that would be a valuable piece of feedback for you, too!

4. **Do your thing**. Now you're ready to use your new behavior as you rehearsed it. And try not to think about the fact that two people are taking notes on everything you do. As if you didn't have enough to worry about before this!

5. **Ask for feedback.** The moment of truth has arrived. You've done your thing and either they're inspired or you've expired, or both. But you're not done yet. One at a time, ask your observers what they think. It's up to you whether you want feedback on the whole experience, or just the new behavior you were working on. Here's a very important reminder—you can specify your wishes to your observers. You can also work it out with them ahead of time if you'd rather receive the feedback in writing, on voice mail, on e-mail, or in person. So many choices! Gee, wouldn't it be swell if we could always control how we get feedback as well as what kind of information we want? If you don't get a response right away, be persistent. The only way for you to improve is to keep asking.

Who invited Sister Ignatius?

What do you do when your observers are giving you feedback? You've probably been on the receiving end of feedback before. For example, Sr. Margaret always used a ruler to help her get her point across. (A very effective mode of providing feedback, but no longer acceptable, thank God.) Pat Heim recalls a negative grade school feedback flashback:

> When I was starting to write *Hardball for Women,* Sister Mary Ignatius showed up on my shoulder. Every time I would write I would hear her berating me. And I literally called the publisher and said I can't do this book, and so I'll be sending back the advance. She said, no, let me put you in touch with a writer. That's when I got hooked up with Susan Golant. We did the book and Susan chased away Sister Mary Ignatius.
>
> Pat Heim, author of *Hardball for Women*
> President of the Heim Group

We hope you realize that cowering and crying aren't the ideal responses to feedback. Dry your tears and stand up straight, or we'll give you something to cry about. Wait a minute, wrong book. Try the following:

a. **Use Active Listening Skills**. Pay attention to what the person is saying. Try to suspend judgement. Work to reduce your own defensiveness. And take a moment to reflect before you respond.

b. **Check Your Understanding**. Make sure you've understood the feedback. Ask questions for clarification, and ask for specific examples. Then try to paraphrase what you heard.

c. **Acknowledge the Feedback**. Let your observer know you heard and understood and that you'll think about the feedback. You don't have to agree with whatever feedback was given, but now is not a good time to get into a debate.

d. **Reflect**. Reflect on the feedback and decide how to integrate the information. Remember that the feedback is not about you—it's about the effect your actions have had on the other person. Look for things you can do to improve or practice further.

e. **Regroup**. Gather all of the relevant information and evaluate the outcome. Define what part of the outcome was right on or right off. Were you a smashing success? Was it a flat-out-didn't-work, or just a less-than-expected result? It's important to have a clear understanding of how the outcome did or didn't match up with your initial expectations. Evaluate your measurements.

How do you define what part of the outcome was right on or right off? You can't just toss out the pieces that make you uncomfortable. But do keep in mind that only about 10 percent of the feedback you receive may be accurate and have merit. The other 90 percent may be merely a personal preference or dislike for your style or methods.

What prevents you from buying 100 percent of the feedback, 100 percent of the time, hook, line, and sinker? How do you know which is the 10 percent to keep? At this point it may be helpful to find a new face to help you sort through the feedback. Find someone in whom you have high confidence and trust. Sit with this person and evaluate the feedback as it relates to the measurements you have set up in advance. Pull out the points that will let you fill in a "score." Work those measures—pump that iron!

If you get a lot of similar feedback on the same issue, investigate further and give it serious consideration. Try to separate the personal from the business/skill-based feedback. The personal feedback usually deals with character traits. When reviewing it, consider the source. Your character may not be in question, but misinterpretations may have occurred. It is your responsibility to try to understand the situation and change how you communicate to better represent yourself. Beware not to take business feedback too personally. Look instead at your skills and focus. Remember the feedback isn't a statement on whether you are a good or a bad person.

Hey...not that button!

Keep in mind that we all have our own personal quirks. And we all have buttons that can be pushed which trigger a flood of emotions disproportionate to the situation. You may hold things near and dear to your heart that, when someone critiques them, you feel attacked, even if that wasn't the observer's intention. Your objective third party will be a big help in these situations. You should be comfortable discussing these hot spots with this person, if nobody else. A Catholic grade school graduate shares one experience with feedback:

I had worked for the same company for three years. Each time my yearly review came up, I was given glowing marks. I got lots of praise from my boss, from my customers, and from my coworkers. Imagine my surprise when my review came due one year and my boss told me he'd like to include the Executive Director in the process. I wasn't even sure the ED knew my name, so why would he want to be joining our discussion? Something had to be up.

To make a long story short, what was normally a 30-minute process turned into a 5-hour session in which both my boss and the ED attacked me from various levels. It turned out that one of my coworkers didn't think I was working hard enough and had spent the previous year campaigning to have me fired. Not only was I surprised at this feedback, but it also seemed very strange to me that I hadn't heard a word of this before. I was shaken to my core. I was working as many as 15 hours a day, traveling all over, being the goodwill ambassador for the company. My customers and other coworkers loved me. Why was one person trying to sabotage me? Worse yet, why were my boss and the ED agreeing with her?

I needed answers, but whom could I trust? I finally decided to confide in someone with whom I had worked prior to my coming to this company, who had worked with all of the players in this scene, but who was not employed by the company. She let me vent, cry, scream, and just get generally frustrated with the whole situation. Most importantly, she listened objectively. She was able to help me figure out that my intentions at work had been good, but that my priorities and that of my coworker were not the same. While I have since moved on from that company, I was able to learn a lot from this painful situation thanks to her help.

Anonymous

Once again, all together now, let's repeat Our First Commandment—*You can't improve the results without improving the process used to generate them.*

Let's go to the Gap®

So what's your next step? You got it, girl. Go back to the steps of the translation process and look for gaps. Did you have all the information you needed? If not, how will you get better information in the future? When you were defining the behavior did you fully understand your Customers? Did you accurately predict what it would involve for you to exhibit the behavior? Were you lined up with organizational policies?

When you find gaps, don't just say, "I'll do it better next time." Make it more formal. Think through how you need to change the process to get better results. Discipline, discipline, discipline. When you find things that work well, don't take them for granted. Make sure you incorporate them into your process for next time. And keep on going. Loop back—all the way back to Challenging your Mindset, or to Defining Behaviors, whatever is appropriate based on your learnings. Fill the data bank in your head with all this rich information you've learned about yourself, about the environment around you, and about how to improve the very process by which you will continue to develop your leadership abilities. Patricia Zander reflects:

> I tend to think a lot. Some would say too much! I am not even aware of the amount of planning, challenging, and anticipating of outcomes I do in

my head. At least not until I am in the situation where the idea emerges. In the past I would go right to the idea and expect everyone to be able to discuss the pros and cons and revel in the excitement of it all. Unfortunately, what usually happened was others felt as if the idea came out of nowhere like a speeding bullet—aimed right at them—especially my more "creative" ideas. Out of nowhere? I don't think so! Because I had already spent huge amounts of time and energy analyzing the situation in my brain, it made total sense to me for many reasons that I thought were obvious.

I found my energy drain as I explained the idea over and over again, until others were comfortable with it and I had lost the opportunity to quickly turn it and spin off of it to generate new ideas. Those around me found this frustrating as well. One day a colleague suggested that I spend more time telling people the thought process I went through leading up to the idea. I felt a tightening in my stomach. That was so much work. But I said I would try. I went through the process of defining how I would do this and tried it out. Feedback I received was very favorable. People felt included, and they were able to evaluate the idea. But I was dying. It was so much work for me to remember my own silent thought process and recount it. It shut down my ability to build rapidly on an idea. It shut down my creativity.

The feedback told me how important and valuable it was for people to understand my thought process and the silent analysis I went through. But I also knew that it was critical that I not severely limit my creativity.

As a compromise, I now try to separate out when communication is really needed and when creativity is most important. When I know my creativity has to be allowed to run wild, I let people know I will cover the behind-the-scenes reasoning later. If it's pure communication that's needed, then I share my thoughts up to the part where I need to create again. This is not a perfect solution, as evidenced by the new bullet holes I see in the wall on a regular basis!

Patricia Zander, CEO/Owner
Oriel Incorporated

Genuflection

Gathering good feedback and pulling out the key insights are absolutely critical for improvement and success. Think of the feedback you've received over your career.

- What valuable information did you get from this feedback?

- What was new information for you?

- What surprised you?

- What really made you mad?

- Can you rethink the negative feedback and pull out the positives from it?

- Who or what can help you stay objective?

Benediction

Earlier we said Catholic girls learn to have faith in things they cannot see. And you were going to turn that faith toward you. Now's the time to turn it on!

Chapter 8

Practicing Behaviors: Why I Should be Pope

• • • • •

*W*hat happens if everything doesn't go well? What if some of your attempts to lead don't work quite like they were supposed to and people don't respond like they should have? It can be very unsettling, to say the least! This happens to everyone, from young Catholic girls to the best of leaders. Unfortunately, as you already know, this is an opportunity for significant improvement. But remember, Catholic girls are tough. We can deal with a little pain.

Experience is what you get when you don't get what you want.

Anonymous

Some experiences do have a significant impact on one's understanding of one's self, one's view of the world, one's sense of right and wrong, and one's subsequent behavior. All experiences are not equal.

Experiences that create lasting change are rarely the product of routine daily fare or of minor turns in an otherwise straight road. The experiences that changed executives were hairpin curves or stomach-turning drops that forced them to look at themselves and their context through a different lens. Transformational experiences almost always forced people to face something different from what they had faced before. In a real sense, the challenge lay in what they weren't really good at, not in what they had already mastered. The harder the test, the deeper the eventual learning, even though for a time afterward, the full significance of the experience might be unclear.

Experiences that have a strong personal impact are almost always loaded with adversity. Because people often prefer to avoid adversity, many of the most developmental experiences happened as a result of fate rather than volition; still others were more or less forced on people by a boss or the organization. Of the experiences entered into willingly, even eagerly, executives sometimes had to admit in retrospect that they hadn't realized what they were getting into—they might not have done it had they known, although having survived it, the experience was invaluable. Experiences that teach are like that.

> Morgan W. McCall, Jr.
> *High Flyers*

Expecting life to treat you well because you are a good person is like expecting an angry bull not to charge because you are a vegetarian.

Shari R. Barr

When you are changing your behavior, try new things on. While you're hanging out there right in the middle of things, "stuff" is going to happen. Even though we all wish we had much less stuff to deal with, the opportunities for learning and improvement are numerous. Does anyone else think that a little less opportunity would be such a bad thing?

Guilt, the gift that keeps on giving

You will find that there is much more going on at this stage than you bargained for. More than your behavior is about to be affected. In working through this process you are defining behaviors and expected outcomes. You predict the outcomes based on your beliefs. But when things don't go as planned, it will cause doubt. We think we want the truth, but we're afraid we can't handle the truth. Panic sets in. What if it's all been for nothing?

You may doubt yourself, your abilities, and what the organization really stands for. You may doubt the values of those around you. And to make things worse, all this doubt and questioning is very difficult for the Catholic grade school graduate. Guilt, guilt, guilt! We

The bottom looks great from here. I think I'll jump.

were never supposed to doubt or question. Well now you are; in fact, now you must. Franny VanNevel tells us about her doubts:

> I remember the first time I missed Sunday mass. I waited all day to be struck dead—literally struck dead. That's how Catholic I was. I was absolutely stunned when nothing happened. As liberating as it

was not to get whacked down by a lightning bolt, it was also very defeating. Now my entire belief system was suspect. If I was still alive after missing mass, what else could I get away with? What else wasn't true?

Franny VanNevel, Writer

With each learning experience you get closer and closer to your own unique style. You're questioning, you're doubting, you're readjusting your view of the world. You begin to branch out and realize that leadership is about choice and using your own free will. It's not about following a script.

Easy to say, but what did you learn in Catholic grade school? Some of us learned we were weak if we doubted. We were to seek forgiveness and never doubt again. But some Catholic girls received much wiser advice. They were told that doubting was good and necessary, for in order to truly have an integrated healthy belief system you had to question, challenge, and develop your own unique set of principles. And they were taught that beliefs should not be closed and static. They should be continuously re-examined and modified based on new knowledge about themselves and their world. They were told that if you could do this you would find peace, wisdom, and free will. And if you still chose God by virtue of free will you were held in even higher regard.

When caught in this kind of crisis at work, you can become your own worst enemy. Paralyzed with insecurity in a world that doesn't make sense, you feel loneliness, self-doubt, fear, and betrayal. Your first instinct is either to go take a nap or stock up on some chocolate. You don't want to go one step farther. You want to get in your jammies and lock the doors. Who needs it?

> *You must do the things you think you cannot do.*
>
> Eleanor Roosevelt

The point of no return

When your Catholic faith got shaken, chances are you could find a friend or a favorite nun or priest to talk to. They helped you sort things out and figure out what to do next. It's much the same for adults, except the stakes are higher. Being in a stage of doubt and questioning is like being in quicksand. Don't hold back; seek out a mentor or read about how other leaders made it through their times of crisis. A mentor can secure the other end of your lifeline. With a mentor, you can limit the burden of learning from your mistakes and you can lessen the bruises. A mentor can help you stay in a position of strength instead of one of defense. Maybe you just need to keep having faith. Maybe you need to adapt your beliefs. Maybe you need to question everything so you can get to a point where you can let things go and move on. Mary Dwyer remembers her own crisis of faith:

> When I was in college, I found out my favorite hometown priest ran away with the parish organist who had just graduated from high school. I was devastated, appalled, and thrilled all at the same time. It turned my belief system upside down. Nothing fit. It took me years to realize he was only

human, probably very lonely, and had opted for a different life. I guess when you're that boxed in, the only way out is by rocket ship.

Mary Dwyer, Vice President/Accounts Supervisor
Lindsay, Stone & Briggs Advertising Incorporated

Each time you get through a crisis you will come out much wiser, more adaptable, more agile, more at peace with yourself, and

You can't change the direction of the wind, but you can adjust your sails.

Anonymous

more able to exercise free will. All pretty good traits for a leader! One thing is for sure: moving up to the world of free will requires you to go through the tunnel to come back out into the light. You are still in control!

Going through serious questioning and doubt to create your own opinions and standards is what gives you the ability to make wise decisions.

You have to develop your own decision-making style, explore your character, and find out what's ticking deep inside you (besides your biological clock). When in doubt, leaders still *do*. The ability to do comes from inside. It's what drives you forward and it's what often drives others crazy.

How do I work? I grope.

Albert Einstein

When you're first starting out, you may not see the big picture. Hey, you might not even see the small one. For the most part you're operating on autopilot. You may feel like you're flying blind, but it's your "self" that's guiding you. You're operating from your character, relying on yourself to get the job done, even though you may not know exactly what you're doing.

Even in the face of doubt and uncertainty, dare to take risks. Keep going. Keep defining behaviors and trying them out. Keep learning and improving. If you fail, fail gloriously. At least you had the guts to try. Losing is really the next best thing to winning—at least you tried, you got in there and mixed it up. Or you got in there and got mixed up. If Einstein said he groped, it's more than okay for us to admit we don't always know if our efforts will be successful. The important thing is to hang in there and dare to give it your best shot. Over time you will gain confidence and begin to realize part of your dream. You will be able to say "I am a leader."

Advances are made by those with at least a touch of irrational confidence in what they can do.

Dr. Joan L. Curcio
Editor

Burned at the High Stakes

Now here is an interesting dilemma. What happens if things work out well? What if you get the expected outcomes? Are you nuts? Yes, thanks very much for asking.

Give the lady what she wants.

Marshall Field's
department store
motto

At first it's natural to attribute every success to luck. It's safer that way. Pure luck. It couldn't be you. "Boy, we sure lucked out this

time. Next time...who knows. They might find me out." You
didn't think you knew what you were doing, but maybe you did.
At the same time every misstep is your fault—remember the Mea
Culpa mindset?

Am I paranoid or is someone following me?

It is normal to be afraid when you start to get what you want.
Hence the old saying: Be careful what you wish for, you just
might get it. As much as you want it, you don't, because you
know with your increasing expertise and success comes more and
more responsibility and even higher expectations. The stakes just
keep getting higher and higher. As a Catholic grade school
graduate you may try to downplay this,
but inside you take this responsibility
very seriously. You're still scared about
screwing up and ruining everything,
and you're still not sure how much of
this is luck. (It couldn't really be you.)
And to make things really bad, now
that you've perfected your leadership
skills people are actually following you! Is there no mercy?

> I don't know anything about luck. I've never banked on it, and I'm afraid of people who do. Luck to me is something else: hard work—and realizing what is opportunity and what isn't.
>
> Lucille Ball

Underneath your passion and enthusiasm is a tiny nagging voice
that's yelling at you to quit raising your hand, quit opening your
mouth, and quit thinking you can do this.

Catholic girls may be even more cautious than others. If you
happen to notice that you are making strides, you may feel like

you'd better shorten your step and
watch for cracks. Catholic girls know
for sure that "Pride goeth before a
fall." The fall equals going to hell. No
thanks. Humility is no big stretch for
the Catholic soul. In measured
amounts it's great. In heavy doses it's
lethal.

> *If I had my life to live over
> again, I'd dare make more
> mistakes next time.*
>
> Nadine Stair
> Author

"Peace be with you" and now go back to challenging your
mindset. Take those beliefs that are causing you anxiety and
challenge them away. Are you uncomfortable because you think
you are not worthy of success? Are you squirming because you
know you are out of the comfort zone
for a woman or are you threatening
someone around you? Do you feel
boastful? Let's go really deep. Are you
turning into one of the money-lenders
in the temple? This old mindset is going
to cause you trouble, and it's a killer to
get over. But keep on truckin'.

> *Don't be humble, you're
> not that great.*
>
> Golda Meir

As you move on in your leadership development, you will likely hit
a time of crisis. When that happens, don't forget one of your best
friends—your sense of humor. (Did you hear the one about the
nun on a bicycle?) Humor makes a great date. Take it with you
wherever you go and people will think you're something special.
Humor and humility make a nice couple, they make parties more

fun and staff meetings more pleasant. They also make a great magic trick. By showing you're not too full of yourself, others dare get close to you, and you dare get close to them. Just think where we'd be if nobody told Ben Franklin to go fly a kite!

> *It's hard to fight the enemy who has outposts in your head.*
>
> Sally Kempton

Remember: if you make a mistake, you can learn from it whether you laugh or cry. Don't know about you, but most women don't look good in a horsehair shirt. We're not into flogging. (Or jogging!) When all else fails, laughter is the best medicine. It's foolish to swallow any other.

> *Always acknowledge a fault frankly. This will throw those in authority off their guard and give you the opportunity to commit more.*
>
> Mark Twain

Whoa! We need a break. Let's stop by the holy water font and say a few Hail Marys. Do you know how far you have come? Do you know how much you have grown? (Remember that we're leaving our thighs out of this.) And believe it or not, our behaviors are now so good we want to make sure we don't lose them. Hallelujah!

But how do you ensure that you will hold on to them? How do you integrate them into your core so they become second nature? How do you ensure deep, lasting change? Do you remember what Sister Maria Juanita taught you? You must practice! Through repetition, specific behaviors become your unconscious response to situations.

Is that the Virgin Mary over there?

There's not a better day in the entire world for a young Catholic girl than her First Communion. The white clothes, the candle, the veil, the shoes, a new medal, the songs, the party, and the money! It was the perfect blend of fervor, fashion, finance, and fun. At seven or eight years old, we were totally pure in mind and spirit and felt as close to the Blessed Virgin Mary and Jesus as we ever would in our lives. All that remained between us and complete salvation was getting the moves right on that special day. We had to make sure we did everything perfectly, no matter how nervous we were.

We remember practicing the steps of our First Holy Communion for months. We pounded through the Baltimore Catechism to make sure we had every passage memorized in case Father Peter showed up to quiz us. We had the vision, and we knew what we wanted to be. We went to church over and over again in order to perfect every movement, every expression. Up the aisle, take the host (remember the fake hosts and the anticipation of getting the real thing?), down the aisle, back to the pew, genuflect, and pray. And we had people there to let us know how we were doing. There was swift retribution. (Ah, yes! Feedback!) Sister Mary Regina ruler-rapped the knuckles of any kids who weren't paying attention. But still, we were out there, doing it. One girl in the class, Suzie, prayed that she'd die right at the communion rail. She said she knew she'd never be as holy as she was that very minute. We all knew she'd go straight to heaven.

Well, the good Sisters weren't so far off. Practice is everything. It's critical. When you practice a behavior and constantly visualize yourself in a situation, you're moving yourself closer to that goal. Patricia Zander takes us back in time to her stint as a musician:

> When I was little I took piano lessons from Sister Rita Claire. I think it was a requirement. I remember sitting at that piano bench, back straight, skirt smoothed over my lap, hands poised over the keys as she watched and waited. All I could hear were the sounds of the metronome and my heart beating, loudly and steadily, not always in synch. I was so intimidated.
>
> Then I would begin playing. Every single time the same thing happened—my left hand followed my right hand in perfect lock step. Sister would gasp. I would stop and try again. The more nervous I got, the more my left hand would clone itself as the right hand. Over and over again. I thought I was going to die. She would end the lesson with instructions to practice, practice, practice. I guess I never practiced enough because Sister eventually put me on her Don't Call list.
>
> Patricia Zander, CEO/Owner
> Oriel Incorporated

Practice in different environments. When you practice the behavior in different situations, you perfect it and make it more robust. Work it over and over again, and soon it will become part of you. In times of crisis when your behavior comes directly from your character, it will be there for you. But as with most things in life, change doesn't happen overnight. It usually takes six months or more for a change to become securely ingrained into your existing system, but once it's there you can rely on it.

Always wear clean underwear

A note about practice. It is human nature to find yourself rationalizing why you don't need to practice today and why you don't really need to make the changes you envisioned in the first place. We can all think of examples of this!

But practice is key for leadership development. Reminders and incentives can keep you going on the right path and keep you practicing. Reminders keep the reasons for practicing in front of you. Some suggestions:

- Put a note in your underwear drawer that reminds you why you are practicing. The up side of this idea is that you are likely to see the reminder every day—clean, white, cotton undies are a staple in our wardrobe, right? If you find yourself pushing the note aside, change messages as the idea may be getting stale. To keep it fresh, you may want to change the note each time you add clean laundry to the drawer.

- Select a family member or trusted friend who will nicely, but regularly, ask you how your practicing is coming along. Making a verbal commitment to someone is a powerful reminder and incentive. Pick someone who will keep your feet to the fire without burning you. Guilt may be the gift that keeps on giving, but it seldom gives the motivation you need to stay on track.

- Pick one or two key words you will likely hear every day that will remind you of the effort you are working on. This can keep the effort fresh in your mind on an irregular, but frequent, basis. Every time someone says, "Thank you," "How are you today?" or "Offer up the pain" you remind yourself of the effort you are working on.

Incentives can come in many shapes and forms. An incentive can be a tangible gift or purchase, but it is really anything that appeals to you or rewards you. This can include time for yourself, simplicity, relaxation. You get the picture. In order to overcome the urge to give yourself too much slack, think of an outcome of your efforts that has high personal value. It may be visible, it may be private. Have an easy and immediate way to remind yourself of this outcome when times call for it. Use it and renew it. It may mean the difference between moving on or settling for less. Some suggestions:

- Treat yourself when practice milestones are reached. You may have a goal of giving others on your team a chance to speak before you draw a conclusion. If you have weekly meetings, it may work well to treat yourself if you make your goal at five team meetings in a row. The treat can be anything that motivates you and feels "special," like buying a CD, relaxing in a hot bath with candles lit, or giving yourself one hour to read a novel.

- Remember to keep a picture in your mind of how the change will feel and what value the action will have as you get closer to making it a new habit. The outcome should have an incentive value itself by improving something in your life or making your job easier. Imagine yourself summarizing the discussion of your team members, rather than jumping in first with your conclusion. Imagine how much more open your team members will be in meetings.

- Ask for feedback from trusted sources. Hearing positive reactions to the changes you are making can be a welcome incentive to keep moving in that direction. You might consider asking the person responsible for reminding you to practice for their impression of how the change is going.

- Provide your own internal incentives. You know, that character thing. Getting yourself aligned with who you really are, what you think, and how you feel is ultimately the best incentive and reward out there.

What is in your future? You can't know what the future will bring, but you can dream about it. Just remember: some of your dreams will be fabulous productions starring You, You, You. Others are going to be nightmares starring You, You, You. Good or bad, at least you're doing something; you're moving. You wake up from dreams. You'll get over your mistakes. The important thing is to keep your goal in sight and keep your heart connected to your dream.

Genuflection

Warning! Don't start making improvements unless you believe you're really ready. Think about something that you've made an improvement on in your personal life—exercising, watching less TV, spending more time with your kids, etc.

- How long did it take to make this improvement?

- Are you still doing it? If yes, what keeps you going in your efforts to improve? What makes you want to stop?

- If you're no longer doing it, what made you stop?

- What was the reward besides feeling better about yourself?

- Who did you tell about it? Who was your support network?

If you are ready to make a change right now,

- How long do you think it will take to make this improvement?

- What will keep you going in your effort to improve?

- What may make you want to stop?

- What will your reward be, besides feeling better about yourself?

- Who will you tell about it? Who will be your support network?

Now you should be able to judge whether or not you're really ready to make this change. If you don't feel ready, what needs to happen to make you feel more ready? When would you be ready? Who can help you get ready?

Benediction

Getting out there and trying is all about courage. The women we learned about in the parables and Bible stories were silently strong. They were courageous. You have that inside of you. It's one of your most precious characteristics. Trust and rely on it.

Part 3

Someone's Leading Lord, Kum Ba Ya

Chapter 9

Teaching and Coaching: Flying Soul-O

• • • • •

We are getting close to the end of examining your growth as a young Catholic girl, and you're about as holy as you're going to get. You are filled to the brim with the Holy Spirit. In fact, you've got enough fervor and desire to be the next Pope. Oh yeah, girls can't be Pope. And here you sit with your faith all aflame.

At work you've started experiencing successes, your comfort margin is increasing and you're picking up momentum. You're happy to take on extra assignments, work late, whatever. You live, breathe, and eat this job! You own this job. You feel valued, and you think your chances are great to go as far as you want to go.

You don't want to sit still and learn anymore, you want to stand up and get busy. You start thinking about how to charge through to that goal. You're so close! You're a force to be reckoned with!

"I'm going straight to the top!"

You know the rules, the rituals, the ins and outs, the ups and downs. You've really progressed with your leadership capabilities and you're bringing in results. It's time to charge ahead and make a difference. But wait! Where is your flock and how are they doing?

Up to this point we have talked a lot about you and your experiences. We have focused primarily on you because when you are learning how to modify and change your behaviors, you needed that self-directed time to focus on your own development. But now it's time to expand your horizons. Think back to the beginning of our journey. We defined a leader as someone who is on a path, in quest of a goal, and who behaves in a way that motivates others to follow and join in the leading.

A leader brings success to the organization by building the talent within. A leader's greatest personal contribution is to develop leaders at all levels of the company. This will not only challenge your leadership capabilities, but also challenge your patience and endurance.

The hills are alive with the sound of music...

It can be very frustrating to be so close to a goal that you can taste it, and yet you have to slow down, regroup, and concentrate on how those you lead are going to reach the goal. They may not share your enthusiasm or excitement. They may not have the skills to go the last mile. But you have the ultimate responsibility to make sure they *do* make it. Remember that the results will be worth it. Today's organizations cannot rest on the laurels of only a few key players; all the members must be key. If the goal is to reach the top of the mountain and sing out to the valleys below, wouldn't you want a full chorus singing?

How do leaders ensure that those they lead will be part of the winning team? They do it through their own behaviors, by interpreting and abiding by the rules according to the situation at hand, by being excellent teachers and coaches, and by communicating a message that will inspire and guide.

Do as I say, not as I do?

What are some of the fundamental behaviors that motivate others to follow? First, others begin to follow when they trust you. According to Stephen Covey, author of *Principle-Centered Leadership*, trustworthiness is more than integrity; it also connotes competence. Before I trust you, I want to know that you're competent as well. In other words, you engender trust by doing what you say you'll do, and doing it with competence. To do this consistently is superhuman, to do it perfectly is impossible. Be prepared for times when no matter how hard you try or want it (and of course pray for it) you can't deliver what you promised. This is when you're most likely to slip back into your days of guilt and unworthiness. But we already know that's really just a cop-out, a way of giving up and lowering expectations for yourself. Is that really how you would want those you rely on to act when they make a mistake? Then you shouldn't act that way either. Instead, pull out the humility, honesty, and trust in others, and communicate from your heart and character. Remember when God closes a door, a window opens. So get over it, and go for the window.

As we discussed before, there is no magic set of ingredients for this type of success. But there is consistency in what people look for in those they choose to follow. Based on a study by James M. Kouzes and Barry Z. Posner, co-authors of *The Leadership Challenge*, in comparing the top characteristics of admired leaders, the same top four characteristics appeared both in 1985 and 1995. According to the study, people seek someone who is:

- Honest
- Forward-looking
- Inspiring
- Competent

Honesty remains the most important characteristic. What people look for and admire is the real thing, and they decide whether you are honest through experience with you. They compare what you say to what you have said you believe. They determine the integrity of your stated values and beliefs by how you behave. What they see is what they get, and they compare it to what they were led to believe. It really all does come down to you leading from your character, your core beliefs, and principles. Even if people don't agree with everything you say, or like everything you do, you will earn their respect if you are honest.

The specifics of being honest will be different for everyone. This is why it is so important to define what it will mean for you, and to try it out. Remember Anne and Teri? They'd both benefit from incorporating honesty, as well as the other attributes, into their process as they learn to lead. In fact, you might want to give these attributes a whirl yourself as you work through the process and see what you find.

Rules are made to be broken

Let's revisit the rules. Leaders often find themselves in situations that are not black and white, and they must interpret a rule or policy for the situation. They know following "good" rules is critical for the stability and success of the organization. But just think of all the rules you have had to follow in the workplace. How many were useful and how many were old baggage from days gone by? And

> *If you obey all the rules you miss all the fun.*
> Katharine Hepburn

think about rules you rebelled against, only to discover later that they weren't so bad. Early in her career, Patricia Zander discovered some rules have merit after all:

> I believed girls would go to hell if they didn't wear a slip. Who could survive the horror of having the light shine behind you and reveal your shape? As I got

older this was definitely a rule to rebel against. But I was to learn it had much more value than I ever imagined. I was working for a company that was experiencing a significant amount of reorganization and downsizing. As a result, my job was continually changing and expanding. I began to fall way behind in compensation relative to my job responsibilities. Because these were my wonder years of self-sacrifice, I was working way beyond the job requirements.

My manager asked to meet with me one day to discuss several things. I sat across the desk from him and laid out the papers relevant to the meeting. At the close he told me I was going to get a raise. It didn't quite bring me up to the lowest level of the job range, but it got me closer. They really wanted to give me more, but the corporate rules placed a ceiling on the percent increase allowed. Even though it was only 25 cents more per hour to get me to the bottom of the pay range, I would have to wait another year. "Have I been doing the work for the last 10 months?" I asked, and added: "Are you expecting me to continue to do this work?" His answers were yes, yes. "Then I am expecting you to pay me for it," I stated matter-of-factly. He deadpanned, "Sorry, there is nothing I can do."

Those were the wrong words. I flew to my feet, grabbed the bottom of my skirt, and pulled it up to my waist to form a big pocket. I was in full flight mode. With one arm I swooped all my papers into my skirt, grabbed it tightly and held it close to my chest. I threw open his office door and marched across the open area of administrative staff and adjoining offices into my office, skirt and head held high. Thank God, I was wearing a slip!

Patricia Zander, CEO/Owner
Oriel Incorporated

A leader has to figure out if the old rules still apply. As much as we learn and are guided by rules, sometimes they're just obstacles to progress.

Go ahead, rock the boat!

We all know both women and men who always play by the rules (at least the ones they like). They're the first ones to say "We can't do it that way" or "We've always done it this way." As if that means anything. Some people get way too comfortable to rock the boat. They don't want to make waves. They don't even want to look over the edge and see what's in the water or over by the shore.

Changing rules can create a very delicate situation because rules often are a double-edged sword. Any good Catholic girl understands how deeply you can internalize the absoluteness of rules. Don't chew the communion host (blood or flames will surely shoot out of your mouth). Unbaptized babies go to limbo. You must not eat meat on Fridays. These rules (and many others) were tattooed on our souls. And breaking these rules meant committing a sin. A big hairy sin.

But there was comfort in all these rules. The blueprint was clear, and you didn't have to think. You just had to obey and you were safe. We relied on these rules as others do. Think back and remember now how you felt when the rules changed. Masticate the hell out of the host, limbo just up and disappeared, and bring on the sirloin. When one woman's beliefs were shaken to the core she said it perfectly, "I hope it's retroactive, so all the poor souls who ate meat on Fridays can get out of hell."

We were so focused on learning the rules and following them to the letter we missed the point of what it all stood for. One of the best examples of this was Confession. There were so many rules, special prayers, a certain way to fold your hands, making sure not to look through those little holes in the screen to see who was on the other side. "Bless me father for I have sinned..." and away we went.

Before we could partake of our First Communion we had to fess up to being bad. Once we reached the Age of Reason we were led to the confessional and encouraged to spill it. Patricia Zander remembers:

> When it was time to go say my confession, I was terrified that my sins wouldn't be bad enough or that I didn't have seven or more sins to confess. I wasn't even sure I'd done something bad enough to count as a real sin, but the assumption was that you had always done something wrong—you just weren't being honest with yourself. And even if you hadn't actually done anything wrong, a bad thought in itself was plenty.
>
> Preparing for confession, I knew I had to have at least seven sins; I thought it was a rule. After examining my conscience, if I could only come up with two or three sins, I'd make some up. Then the next time I went to confession I could say "Bless me, Father, for I have sinned. I lied during my last Confession." That was always a good carryover sin,

and gave me one less to worry about. What a relief. I guess I was so caught up in the rule itself I missed the point.

Patricia Zander, CEO/Owner
Oriel Incorporated

Rules for the sake of rules are never a good thing. A good leader understands the importance of rules and the need to enforce only those that add value. In the workplace it is so easy to lose track. Rules seem to have lives of their own. A leader has to know when and how to modify and eliminate the useless rules. This is scary. It sometimes feels as if chaos and mutiny will become the norm. And it may surprise you how people want to hang on to a rule even if they don't like following it!

Hey, watch this!

It is important that you are a teacher; it shows your commitment to the development of others. It is an opportunity for you to learn, and people learn best how to make tough decisions from the people who have been there. It's not just a good thing to do, it should be your number one job requirement. Pat P. shares her philosophy on mentoring:

I've had several wonderful mentors and I hope that I am a mentor now because that is what I derive energy from. I love watching what I call *Sprouts* grow. I just watch them become more and more strong and beautiful. It's a wonderful thing.

Pat P., VP of HRD
Fortune 100 company

Mentoring is a personalized, rapid learning process that over time helps others focus in-depth on themselves. You will mentor your employees on their behaviors to help them achieve leadership qualities. You'll help them build their knowledge base (statistical thinking, change management, process improvement and management, strategic thinking, etc.). And you'll mentor them on their ability to communicate, coordinate their leadership style with the knowledge base, and translate it all into action where people will collaborate, follow, innovate, create, and implement.

Flattery will get you everywhere

An experienced mentor understands the basics of human behavior and how to assist people as they make personal improvements. They are good diagnosticians and they have a solid understanding of the business and core methodologies. They form a trusted professional relationship with others that will endure time and crisis.

Remember when we discussed how challenging it was to get through difficult experiences and times of doubt? In Chapter 8 we said to seek out a mentor or read about how other leaders made it through times of crisis. A mentor can secure the other end of your lifeline. With a mentor you can limit the burden of learning from your mistakes. In short, you can lessen the bruises. A mentor can help you stay in a position of strength instead of one of defense. Now you are the one offering the support and the wisdom.

Wow. You're just getting used to people referring to you as a leader and now people want to model your behavior? It can be both flattering and overwhelming at the same time to have such an influence on someone's life. Think back to your first few days at your company. You didn't know anyone. Chances are the language and customs were new and different for you, and you felt as if you'd never get up the learning curve far enough and fast enough to be of any use in your new position.

Typically, people who need your mentoring are in the same position. They may have been with the company for a few weeks or a few years, but they are motivated to seek you as a mentor because they realize that you have valuable knowledge.

So what does someone expect from a mentor?

- Honesty
- Objective, caring, and sometimes challenging feedback
- Encouragement to move out of their comfort zone, yet within their capability limits
- An environment of unconditional trust
- Confidence that their best interests are always at the forefront

But honestly, folks...

When you are receiving feedback, as we discussed in Chapter 7, it makes sense to listen and learn. In fact, if we are asking for feedback, we expect the other person to be straightforward and honest in their evaluation of us. So what is expected of you if someone asks you for feedback? Nothing less than a straightforward and honest response. It can be difficult or uncomfortable to give someone feedback that may be perceived as negative, so it can be helpful to use a model. It may feel corny and awkward at first, but once you have included all of the elements in your feedback that are needed by the person you are mentoring, it will make it easier for both of you.

One method of giving feedback includes some standard statements to help give structure to your discussion. The example on the facing page helps illustrate this process.

This is really a very effective method of providing feedback. It allows you to give someone your observations without being accusatory. When practiced and polished, you will reduce the amount of defensiveness that someone receiving feedback may be inclined to feel. You may find it helpful to have your mentor provide you with feedback in this manner.

I meant to do that

Sometimes there is a fine line between a potentially high-impact strategy decision and one that borders on insanity. A mentor's experience and wisdom, as well as their insight about you, can help you determine how close a decision is to either edge. So if you are called upon to be a mentor, how do you help someone distinguish the strategy from the insanity? Easy. By using the information that you have gathered in your career that has

Statement or Lead In	Description	Example
When you...	Describe the behavior using neutral words and phrases. Be objective—do not make judgments or assign blame.	"When you give your opinion first in the meetings you lead..."
It feels as if ...	Tell the other person what reactions or feelings their behavior triggered. And let them know how you or others interpret their behavior.	"...it feels as if you are presenting the one and only answer, or that others' input doesn't matter."
Because...	Be clear about the impact of this behavior. It may be reactions you observed, you heard, or you felt yourself.	"Because you are leading the meeting, others hesitate to speak or hold back their opinions, which can be frustrating. Eventually people may not want to speak at all in your meetings."
It would be helpful...	Tell the other person what alternatives would be helpful. Provide them with a possible course of action.	"It would be helpful if you went around the room and asked others for their opinions first..."
Because...	Tell the other person why you think a change would be more effective.	"...because others would feel as if their opinions were valued. Also, someone else may voice your opinion in expressing their own."
What do you think?	Give the person an open window in which to respond. Listen to the other person's response and be prepared to discuss other options to come up with a workable solution.	"What do you think?"

qualified you to become a mentor. You may be tempted to go back to your old mindset of self-doubt, but now is the time to concentrate on what you *can* do rather than what you *can't* do.

You can help those you mentor weigh the pros and cons of any given situation. You may find yourself with many roles, from idea generator, to cheerleader, to referee, so be prepared to help your protégé in any way you think will be helpful.

If your protégé is in her first job, she will likely be hesitant to make any major decisions without some guidance. In fact, she may endure a difficult situation for longer than necessary because she is afraid of taking risks. This, of course, is exacerbated by our Catholic grade school teachings. One woman who attended Catholic school from first grade through college shares:

> I don't view myself as very much of a risk taker. I think it comes from having a comfort level. I think a lot of Catholic school was sort of following the rules, and I was very, very good at following the rules and getting the answers out of books and things like that. Catholics are built a lot on rules and fear and guilt and compliance, and I can do that very well. I do all those things very well. But I would really encourage a younger woman very differently along those lines—to be more willing to take risks and be more willing to compete in more of a traditional setting.
>
> Roseanne Saunders, VP of Human Resources
> Valley Health System

Obviously taking risks goes against many of the teachings from Catholic grade school. But sometimes you really need to encourage risk taking to move someone off of center or out of a complacent situation.

Don't follow me, I'm lost

Consider what you know about the company. If the person you are mentoring is relatively new to the organization, she will have trouble seeing the bigger picture. She may see some management decisions as arbitrary or erratic. She may view others as conservative and boring. You can help her see the benefits in management decisions when all she can see are the negatives. You can also model good behavior for her so she can see that you are practicing what you preach. (So to speak!)

When you become a mentor, you may be asked to give advice on career moves, how to get recognition, and especially, how to make the correct political moves inside your organization. You may be surprised at how much of this you can do comfortably for yourself, versus how much you are used to doing for other people. Chances are you analyze each situation based on what your mentor taught you, as well as the experiences you've had in the company or in previous jobs, before you make any decisions. The difference now is that you will need to let other people know what you're thinking. The challenge will be to verbalize a process that may have happened instantaneously in your head but that took years to formulate. Susan Fischer shares her process:

> The line between whether you're a mentor or a supervisor isn't always clear. I work with a lot of students, so I'm not necessarily in a role of employment mentor. I try to be helpful in how to handle being one of 43,000 students on campus. I try to be a role model for them. But I am a mentor with staff. There are a couple of staff members

within our division but not in my office who just don't understand how things work. I make a point of going out to have coffee with them, and if it's clear to me there's an opportunity that they are not seeing, I bring it to their attention. I ask if they are aware of the situation and see whether or not they're interested in jumping on the bandwagon. Here's what it looks like, here's what you might want to do if you want to get yourself noticed given the current climate, which seems to change daily.

Susan Fischer, Associate Director of Financial Aid
University of Wisconsin-Madison

Genuflection

Think back to your formative years in the early part of your career. Who was particularly helpful in guiding you or giving sage advice regarding the world of work?

Did you consider them a mentor at the time? Do you now? Why or why not?

What did your mentor do that was most helpful?

How did they become a mentor for you? What made your relationship with them different from your relationships with others in the organization?

How would you respond if someone asked you to be a mentor to them?

How can you best make yourself available to others to become their mentor?

Benediction

Teaching is the most precious gift you can give.

Chapter 10

Delivering Your Own Story: Sharable Parables

• • • • •

hen we were young studying our prayers and our catechism, we learned by parable. We captured the myth, then the myth captured us. Leaders also concentrate on much more than the facts when they tell their stories. Leaders engage people emotionally. Through their stories, or parables, they offer more than the vision, they encourage motivation and the desire for action. Leaders not only inspire, they must teach how to inspire and energize others. They bring the message deep inside so the speaker and the listener are able to process the information with the head and the heart. They form the bridge between themselves and those they are leading.

Leaders create parables about the future of their organization. They share their knowledge about business growth and remaining true to the values and mission of the company. Leaders include their own personal leadership experiences in the context of the organizational goals. Many leaders compare their personal leadership stories to their personal development as youth, providing insight into how early experiences and beliefs shaped who they are and where they are today. By telling their stories as parables, they provide a picture of the past which is vivid and special. They also are putting the journey into a context that allows the listener to personalize the story for themselves so they can connect at a personal level.

In order to create their stories, leaders combine their experiences with their personal opinion of what it takes for the organization to be successful and what it takes to lead others. A leader's story is built through:

- In-depth examination of personal experiences and identification of what has been successful in the past
- In-depth examination of the organization and the business environment to identify the complexity and magnitude of the job which lies ahead (the story must be grounded in reality)
- Clear definition of her vision of the future—what it is and what it will be like for herself as well as others when they get there (The Promised Land?)
- Integration of all these to create the (personalized) main point

Once the experience and vision have been clearly defined, leaders begin to develop their story. They take it out in public and try it out. They obtain feedback and refine the point so it is simple and clear. They communicate passionately, openly, and often. They tell the story over and over, customizing it for the specific audience and situation, until people around them know it intimately.

Patricia Zander tells this story about finally beginning to feel as if she made it:

> It was the first all-company meeting since I had purchased the company. It was very important to everyone that I communicate my vision of what the company represented and where it was going, how I saw the employees in that vision, and who I was. I knew all these people. I had worked with them for years. But now I was the owner. They had accepted me as a peer, but would they doubt my ability to carry off this new role? I was scared stiff. I wanted to prepare my speech to the very last detail, but I found I couldn't write it. Not even an opening line. Whatever I was going to say had to come from deep inside and I couldn't find the words without seeing their faces.
>
> When I was describing my leadership style to them, what came out was a simple story about how two nights before I had gone to an association meeting for women executives to listen to a motivational speaker. As the evening went on, those around me were enthralled with her message. I thought it was predictable and nothing new. Walking out I was mad at myself because I had too many important things to do to waste time like this.
>
> When I got to my car I realized I didn't have any money to pay the parking attendant. I scoured the car, lifted the floor mats, and lo and behold amongst the dead french fries I found enough change. I caught a glimpse of myself in the rearview mirror at that moment. Who was I, so big I knew more than those in the meeting that night, and yet I was on my hands and knees five minutes later digging for gold so I could get my car out of a parking ramp? I was humbled. The next day I pulled out the handouts from the meeting and went over them very carefully, this time with a very different mindset. Sure the points were obvious, that wasn't

the point. The point was doing the obvious. I still refer to those handouts and think about that night's experience.

In a nutshell that story described who I was and how I would try to lead. I thought people would think it was corny and stupid. I thought they would say, "Oh my God, now we've got a crazy, emotional lady running the company." But that's not what happened. They realized I wasn't perfect and that I could admit it to myself and to them. And they realized that I trusted them enough to be vulnerable. They didn't let me down.

Patricia Zander, CEO/Owner
Oriel Incorporated

Conclusion

Back in Catholic grade school, we would all compete to be the best student of the day and to be chosen by Sister Judith to clap erasers. It was the ultimate reward. It felt so good to be "the chosen one," so to speak. And if we were really lucky that day, our best friend was chosen to clap erasers with us. We'd both be covered from head to toe with chalk dust, grinning from ear to ear. But when we got to school the next day we'd have to start being good all over again. There was no carry-over of good deeds from one day to the next. Each day was a new day, filled with messy chalkboards right alongside our challenges and temptations. And Sister Judith had two new "chosen ones" to pick every day. The rewards were great, but short-lived.

And so it is with leadership. One minute you are feeling great because you've led the team that just landed a big contract and the next you're down because one of your projects isn't going as planned. Guess what? You're never done! We said at the beginning of the book that leaders continually grow and learn. And so it is with the entire leadership process. The good news is that with each new experience, opportunity, or problem you will advance a little bit further towards becoming the best leader you can be. You should be proud of the progress you've made. You've come this far. You deserve a pat on the back. Better yet, give yourself the ultimate reward—go and clap erasers!

Benediction

Forward movement comes when the desire to move is greater than the fear that holds us still.

Patricia Zander, CEO/Owner
Oriel Incorporated

Our Parables

During the course of writing this book, we interviewed women from all over the country and asked them to share their Catholic grade school and leadership stories with us. You'll find yourself laughing at some experiences and shocked at others, but mostly you will feel the kinship with these women that we felt as we talked with them. We've arranged them by topic, rather than by speaker, because you can't tell us apart in our uniforms anyway, right?

On What Going to Catholic Grade School Taught Us

I will never go in not prepared for something. That I'm sure came from grade school. And do you remember memorizing? I have a propensity to try to memorize answers before doing a presentation, so I guess that came from there. I wanted to make sure it was all perfect.   —Pat P.

I think the Catholic schools give you a real emphasis on being able to work effectively in a group. Being able to really work effectively with people, being sensitive, being kind, being able to listen, being empathetic and sympathetic are all things that I use in my job as Vice President of Human Resources.
    —Roseanne Saunders

I told the pastor at church that I committed adultery when I was 7. But thinking about that made me realize how easy it was to take responsibility for things that you didn't have to take responsibility for.   —Mary Wagner

With the Catholic stuff, one of my biggest disappointments growing up was we didn't get to be altar boys—no I'm not cleaning the altar! I was just mad a lot. It wasn't fair, and I told my mom it wasn't fair and she said you're right honey, it's not fair but it's the way it is. You don't get to be a priest either. That really sucks, you know?
    —Susan Fischer

A friend of mine is very funny and talented, and yet she wrote in this incredibly stilted style. I was on the phone with her one day and I told her that I didn't think she wrote like she talked, and she really needed to write like she talks. And she said, "I write that way because of Sister Joanna of the Cross."
    —Pat Heim

The teacher had some authority and the principal had some authority, but the principal and teachers were nuns. It was more threatening to be sent to see the priest than to be sent to see the principal. The thought of having to go see the priest terrified me.
    —Angela Prestil

My younger sister really struggles with the fact that I would not be welcome in the Catholic church, and it breaks her heart. The Catholic church does a good job of teaching girls how to live with that tension.
    —Susan Fischer

Both of my children are in ungraded schools that are noncompetitive, completely unstructured schools. And that was a conscious choice after looking at a whole bunch of places, thinking that my children deserved to have a noncompetitive environment for a period of time. That may have something to do with the way I manage people. I hope it is not competitive in that sense of one person having to sit behind another person if you weren't as good in math or something. So who knows how it affected me.   — Pat P.

On Growing Up in Catholic Grade School

In the seventh grade we did a lot of fill-in-the-blank tests. And we were going over the test, mistakes that we had made, and I didn't make very many mistakes but I had one wrong. And so I opened the textbook and there it was, the right answer was the one I had written. So I dutifully raised my hand and the nun asked me to stand up and I said Sister, I don't believe this item is wrong, in the book it says right here. And she said, sit down. And I just said, but it's wrong, it's right here in the book! And she was not interested in hearing it. But I don't think that's uncommon, you're really not encouraged to confront authority.   —Nancy Buechel

I wound up forcing myself to be the best in a lot of things. And there were a lot of rewards for that. I was real crazy about getting holy cards for being the best at something.   —Mary Wagner

Nobody believed that I actually had oranges from the Garden of Eden pressed in our bible at home—those first graders really didn't believe me.
    —Nancy Buechel

The teacher at the end of second grade gave all 50 students straight A's. So the third grade nun had no way of sorting us out, she put us in our reading groups and you could tell who she thought were the dumb ones. I was very ugly and so she thought I was dumb. And that I couldn't read. And lo and behold if I didn't develop a stutter and became unable to read.   —Pat Heim

I went through 12 years of Catholic education—I didn't know anybody who wasn't Catholic, except maybe the people who ran the local grocery store. There's a whole little universe and you didn't realize how far sucked into it you were until you got exposed to other people.   —Mary Dwyer

In school when I got my report card I was told that I failed self-control. And my first instinct was to scream, "What do you mean I have no self-control?"
—Sue Derhammer

On Unique Punishments

In grade school we were put in rows according to our "capability." I remember that I had a classmate named Craig. I was generally in the first row, I have to admit this. But Craig was usually in the last row and he spoke up a lot. And once the nuns told him they were going to put him in "hell." Hell was a broom closet out in the hallway. But what I remember are the screams as he was approaching it because we all thought that was *really* hell and they were taking him there. And then he went behind the door and we all were screaming and he was screaming. Then it got very silent.   —Pat P.

In the seventh grade one of the girls met one of the boys at the movie theater and someone told the nuns. So this boy was called out in the hallway. It's a very old school with big windows and wooden lockers in the hallway. And Sister took Jim—he probably doesn't remember this, but this was sort of imprinted on our brains—but she took him out in the hallway and I believe she was shoving him up against the lockers because you could hear it, you could hear her throttling him. Because he, poor guy, met this girl at the movies. And that girl was a friend of mine, and she never was talked to by the nuns. But he was physically assaulted for not even *going* to the movies with someone, but for accidentally running into someone at the movies.
—Nancy Buechel

I think this was eighth grade with Sister Roberts. There was a whole section in the Baltimore Catechism on how bad divorce is, and that really

many times it's the kids' fault. Well obviously the catechism is written for the kids and it was around how the kids' misbehavior can cause this kind of tension in the family, and then how bad divorce was. And what was so hard was everybody was reading it, and of course these are people you've been with since you were five years old, and they all know your parents are divorced. But then she made me stand up and read it, and in eighth grade we didn't read out loud anymore. And then three times she said, "I don't think we've heard it." And at that point there were kids in the class saying, "Sit down, don't read it anymore." But you never did that. I stood there and I read it and I remember thinking that was her whole mission that year, to publicly humiliate me. But I remember that over and over again...she'd say, "You're not reading loud enough, you skipped a word, you're stuttering, you pronounced it wrong, do it again." It was horrible.
  —Anonymous

In first grade, after lunch apparently some kid threw their sandwich away and didn't eat it. And a teacher found it in the trash, and she knew it was one of us six because we had been sitting at the same table. Somehow they always had a way of knowing. And she berated all of us and we had to stand in front of the classroom. I remember what it was—it was a jelly and bacon sandwich.   —Pat Heim
(Ed. note: I wonder why the kid threw it away?)

When I was in fifth grade, there was a boy in my class who didn't behave and I guess he must have been pretty bad. As a punishment for him, they brought in a highchair and made him sit in it in the back of the room. This is the kind of stuff that we saw that was going to happen to us. Eventually this kid got shipped off to public school. You see enough of this in your formative years so you learn you have to play by the rules, and if you do things the right way you'll be successful.   —Julie Herfel

The nuns weren't very fun.   —Pat Zander

On Our Favorite Nuns

Sister Mary Alice was my favorite nun. You have no idea how old they are or what they really look like or what they're shaped like.   —Pat P.

Sister Mary Daniel was wonderful because she liked me. She encouraged me and she wasn't crabby at me and I didn't have to share a desk. You can use Sister Mary Daniel's name but you better not use Sister S. because she might hurt some of my family members.   —Nancy Buechel

It has been said that our lives are shaped by those who love us and those who refuse to love us. Those women loved us, and there is no doubt that their affection shaped our lives. They demanded that we always do our best and convinced us that an "A" in Application was the most important grade on the report card. They expected us to be responsible and trustworthy.   —Ann Myers

In retrospect I think about how terrifically strong the nuns were. They had to live in the world but they weren't of the world. And what a struggle it must have been for a great many of them, yet they had the greatest responsibility they could have. They had the education of young children in their hands. I would not change my upbringing in any way, shape or

form. I could not have asked for a better education. I could not have asked for better teachers. I'm a great lover of nuns. I think nuns are terrific.
　　—Mary Dwyer

My messages were inconsistent, sometimes they were crappy and sometimes there were nuns that were just fabulous. And I think one positive thing about being raised Catholic and especially going to Catholic school is that some of the nuns—and I know that wasn't everybody's experience—were fabulous role models for girls. Here you have this strong woman saying, "This is what I want, I did this because I wanted it, not because my parents wanted it, I didn't have to do this." They chose a road that was clearly not of the mainstream.　—Susan Fischer

I remember when Sister Paula got married and I thought she was going to be struck down. She was my first grade teacher and I thought she was the best.　　—Angela Prestil

There was one nun in particular who was very instrumental in telling me it was okay to question the church. Sister Jean Smith taught me to always be true to yourself. And that was a real dawning for me. And to this day I think what a wonderful woman she was.　　— Mary Dwyer

You know, there were points when the nuns were incredibly compassionate. I remember losing my rosary—do you remember you had to say the rosary the first thing in the morning? And I lost it and I was crying and one of the nuns, not my teacher but some other nun, took me aside and gave me her rosary. So there was a great deal of compassion as well, but just in a very structured environment. And I was determined to do well because that was the way I figured they'd love me or they'd like me.　　—Pat P.

On Myths and Rules We Learned

Do I remember having to follow a lot of rules? I hate to say this but that's a dumb question!   —Pat Heim

For five dollars you could adopt a "pagan baby" and you got this card with Mary, Jesus, or somebody on it and inside it was written that you got to name your pagan baby. My parents had always let us earn our way, and if you wanted to do something it's fine except you have to use your allowance and you have to earn the money. Third grade right, you know, go out and do what? Vacuum and dust and vacuum and dust and do household chores up the wazoo until I had my five dollars and by God, I went and I got my pagan baby and I named him John. And so then our year in Kansas ended and my father got transferred to Bangkok, Thailand, where I went to school with the pagan babies.   —Susan Fischer

If you had general responsibilities for the children, which most women did, then taking responsibility for the health of their soul went right along with regular brushing.   —Mary Wagner

When you get your period it's because your womb is crying because it's empty.   —Susan Fischer

We were always seated from smartest to dumbest. First person, first row was the smartest kid and last person, last row was always James W. And for those people in the further rows, I mean for them to just sit there all day long and see how others perceived their intelligence or supposed lack of. And James W. became an inventor, so he wasn't dumb.
—Pat Heim

You really can't point your hands down when you're walking up to Communion because that means you're going to hell.
   —Nancy Buechel

My mother said to me, "You know you're going to get pregnant if you go to the public high school." I didn't know how you got pregnant at that point, so I was wondering if it was in the water there.
   —Pat Heim

Never sit on a boy's lap unless there is a telephone book in between the two of you.   —Nancy Buechel

If you're really a good girl, your guardian angel will reveal himself to you one night in your dreams.
   —Susan Fischer

My husband grew up Catholic, too. And there was one time when we both were having really bad headaches but we didn't tell each other and we were both thinking brain tumor. And finally one night I told him I'd been having really bad headaches and I was wondering if I had a brain tumor. And his response was "No, I think I have a brain tumor. I've got it." It would always be pretty holy to die of something as dramatic as a brain tumor.
   —Julie Herfel

I dislocated my shoulder and the physical therapist was pushing it back in PT, and she told me to tell her when it hurts. And I'm hearing this nun say "Offer up the pain." And I'm thinking jeez, I still hear those little voices sometimes. I'm in therapy thinking, yeah, I can take a little more pain before I pass out.   —Mary Wagner

I remember when I was 10 years old I was a huge fan of the Beatles—it was in the mid-60s. I also remember not understanding about where babies came from or sex, but I do remember the church

On Mentoring or Coaching Others

> I discovered, actually this was probably about five years ago, that one of the chairs in my office has been labeled as the crying chair because everyone who works here at some point has sat in that chair and cried.   —Nancy Buechel

> I ask my daughter who her best friend is and she won't tell me. She says, they're all friends in different ways, Mommy.   —Pat P.

● ● ● ● ●

Share Your Parables

When we interviewed women for this book, we heard story after story about growing up in Catholic grade school. Each woman had her own experience, and each story brought up the memory of another experience. The women who reviewed the book for us wrote stories in the margins of the book before they returned their copies to us. As we spoke with women around the country while publicizing the book, they also chimed in with their stories. Every one was told with a sense of nostalgia, along with a touch of pride for having survived it all.

Do you remember when Sr. Dorothy made Steve R. wear a skirt after recess because he got his pants dirty? What about the time that Sr. Carol sat with you during penmanship to help you form your letters? Does reading all of these stories bring back memories for you? Well, now is your chance to tell yours. Along with your story please include your name, address, e-mail address, and phone numbers so we can obtain the proper permission to use your stories. We'd love to hear from you. Who knows, maybe you'll be quoted in our next book!

Product Manager
Leadership Development for CGS
Oriel Incorporated
Fax: 608-238-2908
E-mail: cgstories@orielinc.com

● ● ● ● ●

Appendix

Genuflections

Chapter 2   The Leadership Role: Nun of the Above

Because you're ultimately responsible for becoming the kind of leader you envision, let's start by reflecting on how swell you are.

- What are your best qualities?

- What qualities do you least like about yourself?

- How will your best qualities *help* you as a leader?

- How will your least desirable qualities *hinder* you as a leader?

- Who are your "Patron Saints" of work? What do you admire or appreciate about them?

- Imagine you are the CEO. One of your key executives is *you* as you are today. How would you as the CEO go about leading *you*? What would it be like to work with *you*?

Chapter 3   Leadership Potential: Follow the Glow-in-the Dark Rosary

Complete the following sentences with the first thing that pops into that little pony-tailed head of yours:

- In grade school, my favorite nun was _____ because she...

- If I had told my fourth grade teacher I was going to grow up to be an important leader at work she would have thought...

- The first time I was a leader was when I...

- In grade school, I was disappointed when I wasn't asked to lead...

Chapter 4 Challenging Beliefs: Suffering Makes You Grow, Which is Why I'm a Size 18

Go through the list of beliefs and adages in the tables on the following pages. Think about what each of them meant to you as a young Catholic girl. Now look at your life and work today. What about those old beliefs is still worthwhile? Can you take some pieces of your old beliefs and make them work for you today? What pieces do you need to leave behind in order to be successful today? Feel free to add a few of your own beliefs to this list.

Belief or Adage	What did it mean to you as a Catholic girl?	Convert the meaning to make it useful in the workplace
God doesn't give you more than you can handle		

Belief or Adage	What did it mean to you as a Catholic girl?	Convert the meaning to make it useful in the workplace
Confess your sins		
God will strike you dead for your sins		

Belief or Adage	What did it mean to you as a Catholic girl?	Convert the meaning to make it useful in the workplace
Divine intervention		
Don't hide your light under a bushel basket		

Belief or Adage	What did it mean to you as a Catholic girl?	Convert the meaning to make it useful in the workplace
Suffering makes you grow		
Add your own		

Chapter 5   Seeking Knowledge: Lead Me Not Into Temptation, I Can Find the Way Myself

Pull out the photo album in your memory. Open up the album and find the snapshots in your mind that depict the following:

You working very hard to do well.

- Why did you want to do well?

- How did it feel when you were working on this goal?

- What did it feel like when you were done?

People challenging you to be better or work harder.

- Who challenged you the most?

- How did their challenging affect you?

- Did you ever forgive them?

- Did you ever thank them?

You fell short or did not perform well.

- Did you survive it?
- How did you feel at the time?
- What effect did it have on you?

People who seemed to help bring out the best in you.

- Who were those people and how did they bring out your best qualities?
- What were the similarities between those people, if any?

Chapter 6   Using the Process:
Becoming a Smarter Martyr

Take some time to fill out your own SIPOC diagram using one of the outcomes below that would be appropriate for displaying one of your new leadership characteristics. Think through the scenario and evaluate how your innate character and core beliefs will influence your behavior. Set a goal for what you want the outcome to be. Decide which behaviors will be most effective. Remember, this isn't imitation or following a script. You should be focusing on exhibiting behaviors that come from your unique leadership style.

My desired outcome is to:

- Operate from a basis of respect

- Model desired behaviors

- Be decisive

- Use humor appropriately

- Encourage others to take risks

- Show my vulnerability

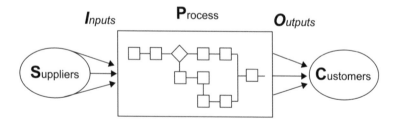

S = Suppliers

Suppliers are people or places (sources) where you can get information about yourself and the environment. Your Suppliers may be:

- You
- Your assistant
- A mentor
- Your boss
- Those you supervise
- Books

- Trainers
- Coaches
- Friends
- Reports
- Your job description
- Personal assessment results

My Suppliers are:

I = Inputs

Inputs consist of relevant information about yourself and the environment. This is the type of internal and external information discussed in Chapter 5. For example:

- Results from leadership style assessments
- Feedback
- Your own insights
- Corporate directives
- Organizational policies
- Description of job duties

My Inputs are:

P = Process

Process is the sequence of steps you go through to turn the Inputs into Outputs. For the Translation Process it's how you take what you know and come up with your best idea for a desired behavior.

My Process is:

O = Outputs

An **O**utput is the desired behavior.

My Outputs are:

C = Customers

Customers are the recipients of your service, behavior, or actions.

Your Customers may be:

- You
- Those you lead
- Vendors
- Your banker

- Your boss
- Stockholders
- Board of directors
- The purchasing customer

My Customers are:

Chapter 7   Feedback: Never Do Cartwheels in a Skirt

Gathering good feedback and pulling out the key insights are absolutely critical for improvement and success. Think of the feedback you've received over your career.

- What valuable information did you get from this feedback?

- What was new information for you?

- What surprised you?

- What really made you mad?

- Can you rethink the negative feedback and pull out the positives from it?

- Who or what can help you stay objective?

Chapter 8   Practicing Behaviors:
Why I Should Be Pope

Think about something that you've made an improvement on in your personal life—exercising, watching less TV, spending more time with your kids, etc.

- How long did it take to make this improvement?

- Are you still doing it? If yes, what keeps you going in your efforts to improve? What makes you want to stop?

- If you're no longer doing it, what made you stop?

- What was the reward, besides feeling better about yourself?

- Who did you tell about it? Who was your support network?

- If you are ready to make a change right now, how long do you think it will take to make this improvement?

- What will keep you going in your effort to improve?

- What may make you want to stop?

- What will your reward be, besides feeling better about yourself?

- Who will you tell about it? Who will be your support network?

Now you should be able to judge whether or not you're really ready to make this change. If you don't feel ready, what needs to happen to make you feel more ready? When would you be ready? Who or what can help you get ready?

Chapter 9   Teaching and Coaching: Flying Soul-O

Think back to your formative years in the early part of your career.

- Who was particularly helpful in guiding you or giving sage advice regarding the world of work?

- Did you consider them a mentor at the time? Do you now? Why or why not?

- What did your mentor do that was most helpful?

- How did they become a mentor for you? What made your relationship with them different from your relationships with others in the organization?

- How would you respond if someone asked you to be a mentor to them?

- How can you best make yourself available to others to become their mentor?

Glossary

Ashes   Distributed as a reminder of human mortality on Ash Wednesday, the first day of Lent.

Baltimore Catechism   A series of teachings from which every child prior to Vatican II learned about the Catholic religion.

Bride of Christ   Another name for a nun. A nun marries the church, and therefore Christ, rather than a human being.

Catechism   The teachings of the Catholic religion, especially to children.

Chapel veil   Prior to Vatican II, all females were required to cover their heads upon entering the church. A chapel veil, or mantilla, was a small square of lace that was bobby-pinned to the head to serve such a purpose.

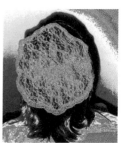

Communion rail   The physical barrier that surrounds the altar and sanctuary designed to show a definitive division between the congregation and those celebrating the mass. No one was allowed beyond the communion rail unless they had an active part in the mass.

Confession The sacrament a young person begins in fourth grade where she personally tells her sins to a priest. The priest acts as a substitute for Christ, absolves the sins, and assigns penance for the wrongdoings in a quantity suitable to the severity of the sins. Mortal sins require more penance than venial sins. Good Catholics go to confession once a month.

Confiteor A part of the mass in which you confess your sins individually by saying this prayer with the whole congregation. The confiteor is named from the first word of the original Latin version, which means, "I confess."

First Communion The sacrament in which a child receives communion for the first time, acknowledging full acceptance of the church's teachings. Normally, children make their First Communion in second grade.

First Friday Attending mass on the first Friday of the month was non-obligatory. Christ allegedly appeared to Sr. Mary Margaret Alocoque from 1673-75. He told her that if you received communion the first Friday of each month, spent an hour in the presence of the Blessed Sacrament each Thursday, and annually celebrated the Feast of the Sacred Heart, you would not die in sin and Christ would be your refuge at the hour of death. In the 1960s, some felt that attending nine First Friday masses in a row would help abolish communism.

Genuflect

Genuflect means "on bended knee" and it is a sign of reverence, respect, and greeting. Upon entering and exiting your pew at the beginning and end of mass, you kneel on one knee and make the Sign of the Cross.

Hail Mary

A prayer said to honor Mary, the mother of Jesus. Priests often assign praying the Hail Mary as penance to atone for your sins after confession.

Holy cards

A small card with the likeness of Jesus, Mary, or patron saint of some particular cause. Holy cards typically have a picture on one side and a prayer on the other dedicated to the person depicted on card.

Holy Days of Obligation

Special feast days celebrating various events in the church calendar. Attendance at mass is required on Holy Days of Obligation.

Holy water   Blessed water used to transfer a priest's blessings to the congregation, thereby remitting venial sins. Also used for the same purpose upon entering the church when making the Sign of the Cross.

Holy water font   The basin used to hold holy water. It is often used for baptisms.

Horsehair shirt   A shirt made of horsehair, which itches incredibly, especially when worn in the summer time. It was supposed to be worn as penance, and you were supposed to offer up the pain and discomfort to the poor souls in purgatory.

Host   Round pieces of unleavened bread distributed at communion.

Indulgences   Penance that is done to make up for sins you have committed. The debt that you owe after your sins are forgiven can only be forgiven with an indulgence. The value of indulgences adds up, and the goal is to get as many as possible to ensure prompt entry into heaven.

Kneeling on jacks   As a form of penance, you had to kneel on jacks and then you were supposed to offer up the pain to the poor souls in purgatory.

Last Rites

Also known as Extreme Unction or the Anointing of the Sick, this is the sacrament Catholics receive prior to their death. It is a final blessing to absolve sins to prepare you for entry into heaven.

Lent

The forty days preceding Easter. They symbolize the 40 days Jesus spent fasting and praying. During Lent, the church emphasizes penance and self-sacrifice in preparation for Easter.

Limbo

Prior to Vatican II, the church believed that anyone who was not baptized Catholic could not make it into heaven, because in addition to any sins you may have committed in your lifetime, you also had the mark of original sin on your soul. Also, babies who had not yet been baptized were believed to go to limbo where they had to wait until enough people on earth prayed for their entry into heaven.

Mantilla

See Chapel veil.

May Crowning

As part of the celebration of May Day, traditionally the kick-off to May—the month of Mary—one young girl was chosen to lead the procession to the church. Once at the church, the girl placed a crown of flowers on Mary's head. In many Catholic schools, being chosen to crown Mary was a great honor.

Medals	A small object with the likeness of a saint who bears the same name as the medal holder or who is the patron saint of some particular cause. 

Mortal sin	A word, action, omission, thought, or desire that is seriously wrong, that you know is seriously wrong, that you have fully consented to committing, and that you actually commit or think about committing on a regular basis.

Original sin	God offered Adam and Eve friendship and immortality so they could enjoy the Garden of Eden forever, as long as they didn't eat the forbidden fruit from one particular tree. Because they ate the fruit, we all lost the bonuses of friendship and immortality.

Pagan babies	Unbaptized babies were known as "pagan babies." By "buying" pagan babies, children helped support missionaries who would then baptize these babies so they could get into heaven. Buying pagan babies would also earn a child an indulgence.

Patron saints	A saint that is designated as the primary recipient of prayers for a specified cause, event, location, item, etc. (For example, St. Patrick, patron saint of Ireland; St. Jude, patron saint of hopeless causes; St. Anthony, patron saint of lost items.) 
Penance	The prayers you must say after going to confession to atone for your sins.
Plenary indulgence	Full remission. If you gain a plenary indulgence and die immediately afterwards, you would immediately go to heaven.
Purgatory	If you die with minor or venial sins on your soul, or with your sins forgiven but unatoned, you go to purgatory instead of heaven or hell. You will stay in purgatory until enough people on Earth have prayed or suffered for you.

Sacrament

An act that changes the recipient permanently. No sacrament, if properly received, is revocable. There are seven sacraments which are intended to be visible acts of worship established by Jesus: Baptism, Eucharist (Communion), Reconciliation, Confirmation, Matrimony, Holy Orders, and Anointing of the Sick.

Sacristy

The room next to or behind the altar that houses the priest's vestments and other accoutrements required to celebrate mass. The priest prepares for the mass in the sacristy.

Scapular

Designed to be worn as an outward sign of your faith, a scapular consists of two little stamp-sized pieces of cloth, often laminated with a saint, Jesus, or Mary on them, joined with two pieces of string. It was developed from the habits of monks in the Middle Ages, which consisted of a tunic and a scapular that hung over the shoulders like a narrow poncho.

Stations of the Cross A series of 14 steps which replicates Jesus' journey through his crucifixion and resurrection. Also called "The Way of the Cross," the stations each have a cross, and often have pictures or sculptures depicting what happened at each stage of the journey.

Tabernacle The cupboard-like storage unit on the altar that contains blessed hosts for communion.

Vatican II The Second Vatican Council, held in 1965. A Vatican Council is a meeting of all the bishops around the world, which is convened by the Pope. The decisions and decrees of the great councils are authoritative and can change the way the church conducts itself. Vatican II is especially remembered for such radical changes as masses being said in the parish's native language rather than Latin, and nuns beginning to use their given name and forego their traditional habit.

Venial sin A sin in which the evil wasn't seriously wrong, or, even if it was, you understood it to be only slightly wrong or you didn't fully consent to it.

Vestments The traditional clothing that priests wear to say mass. The vestments are allegedly patterned after the clothing that was worn in Jesus' time.

Vocation day   While Catholic children are always supposed to be open to the thought of becoming a priest or nun, once a year a special "recruiting day," more popularly known as vocation day, is held in Catholic grade schools to encourage religious vocations with a little more vigor than usual.

References

Leadership References

Cashman, Kevin. *Leadership From the Inside Out.* Provo, UT: Executive Excellence Publishing, 1998.

Covey, Stephen R. *Principle-Centered Leadership.* New York: Fireside, 1992.

Covey, Stephen R. *The 7 Habits of Highly Effective People: Powerful Lessons in Personal Change.* New York: Fireside, 1990.

Essi Systems, Inc. *StressMap, Personal Diary Edition: The Ultimate Stress Management, Self-Assessment and Coping Guide.* New York: Newmarket Press, 1991.

Harragan, Betty Lehan. *Games Mother Never Taught You: Corporate Gamesmanship for Women.* New York: Warner Books, 1978.

Heim, Pat and Susan K. Golant. *Hardball for Women: Winning at the Game of Business.* New York: Plume/Penguin, 1993.

Kouzes, James M. and Barry Z. Posner. *The Leadership Challenge. How to Keep Getting Extraordinary Things Done in Organizations.* San Francisco: Jossey-Bass, 1995.

Kroeger, Otto and Janet M. Thuesen. *Type Talk at Work.* New York: Dell Publishing, 1992.

Kroeger, Otto and Janet M. Thuesen. *Type Talk: The 16 Personality Types that Determine How We Live, Love, and Work.* New York: Dell Publishing, 1988.

Lundin, William and Kathleen Lundin. *Working with Difficult People.* New York: American Management Association, 1995.

McCall, Jr., Morgan W. *High Flyers: Developing the Next Generation of Leaders.* Boston: Harvard Business School Press, 1998.

Markova, Dawna. *The Open Mind: Exploring the 6 Patterns of Natural Intelligence.* Berkeley, CA: Conari Press, 1996.

Markova, Dawna. *The Art of the Possible: A Compassionate Approach to Understanding the Way People Think, Learn, and Communicate.* Emeryville, CA: Conari Press, 1991.

Orlick, Terry. *In Pursuit of Excellence: How to Win in Sport and Life Through Mental Training.* Champaign, IL: Leisure Press, 1990.

Quinn, Robert E. *Deep Change: Discovering the Leader Within.* San Francisco: Jossey-Bass, 1996.

Rosener, Judy B. "Ways Women Lead." *Harvard Business Review.* November-December, 1990, pp. 119-125.

Salmansohn, Karen. *How to Succeed in Business Without a Penis: Secrets and Strategies for the Working Woman.* New York: Three Rivers Press, 1996.

Thomas, Kenneth W. and Ralph H. Kilmann. *Thomas-Kilmann Conflict Mode Instrument.* Tuxedo, NY: XICOM, Inc., 1974.

In addition to these sources, you may also wish to investigate your personal leadership and interaction styles with the help of a local psychologist. We recommend the Myers-Briggs Type Indicator®, the Campbell Interest and Skills Inventory, and the California Psychological Inventory™. These instruments can assess behavioral characteristics, as well as perception, judgement, information gathering, and decision-making styles.

Catholic References

Cascone, Gina. *Pagan Babies and Other Catholic Memories.* New York: St. Martin's Press, 1982.

Dollison, John. *Pope-Pourri.* New York: Fireside, 1994.

Johnson, Kevin Orlin. *Why Do Catholics Do That?: A Guide to the Teachings and Practices of the Catholic Church.* New York: Ballantine Books, 1994.

Meara, Mary Jane Frances Cavolina, Jeffrey Allen Joseph Stone, Maureen Anne Teresa Kelly, and Richard Glen Michael Davis. *More Growing Up Catholic.* Garden City, NY: Doubleday, 1986.

Meara, Mary Jane Frances Cavolina, Jeffrey Allen Joseph Stone, Maureen Anne Teresa Kelly, and Richard Glen Michael Davis. *Growing Up Catholic: An Infinitely Funny Guide for the Faithful, the Fallen, and Everyone In-Between.* New York: Doubleday, 1985.

Stivender, Ed. *Raised Catholic (Can You Tell?).* Little Rock, AR: August House, 1992.

Warner, Karen. *What's So Funny About Being Catholic?* New York: HarperPerennial, 1994.

Index

The Oriel Story

In the Middle Ages, castles were designed with a large, projecting bay window positioned high atop a tower, solidly jutting out from the castle foundation. This window, called an oriel, gave the leaders a view of the vast environment around them. The advantages gained by this perspective were many: From the oriel the leaders could view the progress of work, design roads and create maps, determine if enemies were attacking, or simply reflect on all they were a part of.

Oriel, the company, offers you a wide perspective from a distinct vantage point allowing you to expand your vision, link it to strategic goals, and implement it with the view of the entire system.

In order to bring Oriel to life, we built on the foundation of Joiner Associates, expanding our areas of expertise with the same dedication to excellence that characterizes our data-driven and team methodologies. As a result, Oriel is a flexible, multi-faceted organization that is dedicated to working collaboratively with you to help you Unleash The Potential.™

Oriel Business Groups

Oriel has four areas to help increase your ability to find success in business. Each has a distinct personality offering different means to achieve your goals.

Reality-Based Management™ Group

Services and products that focus on rigorous, data-driven methodologies to promote effective decision making.

Economic Impact Assessment: A consultant works with your team to identify the economic impact of future projects. Our consultants are very experienced in determining the impact of proposed manufacturing plants on community employment, taxes, infrastructure, and demand for services and housing.

Defect-Free Process Design: A combination of state-of-the-art methods based on six sigma approach and problem-solving techniques to enable you to improve process performance and reliability.

Designed Experiments: Learn how to carefully and methodically change how work is done so you can determine the optimal settings needed to improve quality, shorten cycle time, improve market share and reduce costs. Designed experiments are the secret to finding the optimums quickly, accurately, and effectively.

Statistical Process Control (SPC): With SPC, your organization can employ relatively simple tools and methods to systematically collect and display data from processes to better understand and reduce variation—the fundamental building block to real, sustainable improvement.

Process Modeling & Simulation: Gain the edge by learning to develop realistic computer models of business situations to test various "what-if" scenarios. Modeling and Simulation allows you to determine the optimum operating conditions and invest only in those solutions that provide the highest return and lowest risk.

Management Reporting: Managers will learn the key drivers of financial results for which they are responsible and how these drivers affect other parts of the organization. Through a customized system of measurement and reporting, executives and managers can identify, track, and improve the essential elements that significantly impact business results.

Data Analysis and Mining: We will help you find and understand the complex relationships in your corporate databases. And then use these relationships to find invaluable insights into how customers behave, allowing you to predict and meet their needs.

Joiner ® Core Methodologies Group

Services and products that enable organizations to build and implement the management system, methods, and tools they need to exceed customer expectations and achieve business objectives.

Fourth Generation Management: The New Business Consciousness. Brian L. Joiner describes how a new synthesis of management principles can create rapid, sustained improvement.

Fundamentals of Fourth Generation Management. An 8-module video program that explores the basic principles of quality, data, and teamwork. The program mixes video instruction with real-time exercises that emphasize key points and skills.

The Joiner 7 Step Method™. This structured approach to problem solving will help teams and individuals uncover the real issues and develop solutions that are right on target. Available component  products include a hands-on workbook, a storyboard on disk to present your learnings, and **Guiding Succesful Projects**, a quick guide that presents key questions for checking progress.

People & Change: Planning for Action. A straightforward three-step guide that balances instruction and action and provides easy-to-use methods and forms to create implementation plans that secure employee commitment.

Plain & Simple® Series. Guides that teach users how to decide what tools to use in a situation, how to collect the right kind of data, create the charts, interpret the information, and put it to use. The 10 titles include:

Introduction to the Tools   How to Graph
Data Collection   Pareto Charts
Flowcharts   Individuals Charts
Time Plots   Scatter Plots
Frequency Plots   Cause-and-Effect Diagrams

Running Effective Meetings. Learn how to make meetings more productive. This 4-hour instructional program is designed to help any kind of group learn and practice effective meeting skills.

The Team® Handbook Second Edition. This best selling book covers the fundamental skills necessary for teams to be successful. Conflict resolution, problem solving, discussion management, sponsor and management responsibilities are just a few of the skills covered. A set of 212 color overhead transparencies is also available.

The Team Memory Jogger™. A handy pocket guide written from the team member's point of view. This reference is valuable for improving team effectiveness, providing practical tips on feedback skills, having effective meetings, dealing with common team problems, and more.

The Team® Trail Guide. This CD-ROM is designed for team leaders who are new to the role, as well as those who have been learning as they go. It contains team leadership scenarios and examples about teams, roles and responsibilities, 7 keys to successful teams, components of effective team communication, and an 8 step conflict resolution plan.

Voices into Choices: **Acting on the Voice of the Customer**. This how-to book contains an easy to follow information gathering and decision-making process to help you truly understand customer needs.

Core Group Consulting Services

Our consultants are experienced professionals dedicated to helping you maximize your resources. They have worked in their respective fields for a decade or more, helping organizations achieve world-class performance. They are carefully selected to match your situation and work collaboratively with you to solve your problems, improve your business, and exceed your customers' needs.

We are committed to helping you build your capabilities in a manner that allows you to maintain ownership of all improvements, assuring your ability to move ahead independently. We provide practical, directly applicable methodologies that lead to measurable business results. Oriel Core Group consultants bring expertise in the areas of:

Change Leadership
Customer Focus
Employee Feedback Systems
Internal Expert Development
Labor/Management Relations
Lean Manufacturing
Measurement
Organizational Culture
Problem Solving
Process Improvement
Process Management
Six Sigma
Team Building and Facilitation
Training Design
Variation
Workplace/Shop Floor Management

Meeting the Challenge™ Group

These services take you to the very core of your character—where your fundamental leadership abilities reside. Through inventories, questionnaires, personal challenges, practice, and feedback, you'll be fully exposed to the signature pieces of who you are and how you lead. You'll simultaneously feel the tension and experience the power of the challenge. You'll be exposed to the essential tools that are necessary to become the best. The Master Craftsman Series offers the following services:

Leadership Unleashed. Profiles your skills and core competencies to identify the principles and character traits that define your unique leadership potential.

Executive Coaching. 1:1 attention that will challenge, nurture and expand your envelope. They will provide advice and feedback to help you define the critical knowledge to translate who you are into what you do.

Individual Performance Management. A process to help you identify required core competencies and develop a plan with personal performance goals.

Growing Your Executives. Your effectiveness as a leader is measured by how well your people are doing. Learn how to simultenously do your job and develop your internal leadership base.

Building a Cohesive High-Impact Leadership Team. Take the collective talents of team members and merge their distinct personalities into a lean, focused, and highly effective force.

Care & Feeding of the CEO. Learn how to effectively work with and support your CEO.

Organizational Audit. Take a point-in-time analysis of the awareness and functional levels of the organization to identify the pressure points and untapped opportunities.

Developing Leadership from Within. Identify and create an internal system that sustains leadership development within your organization.

The products, services and attitude needed to thrive in Extreme Business™.

For some of us, the world of extreme sports captures our hearts and imagination; we also thrive in the world of Extreme Business. We know that achieving success requires more than just the tried and true. It's about taking risks. Blazing trails. Accepting the knocks, and reveling in the successes. It means you are out on the *bleeding edge.*

You bleed because you are always pushing the envelope and you're prepared to experience the consequences. You live on the leading edge because that is where you revitalize and innovate. You crave the company of others like you and you thrive in a team that challenges and dares to stretch the imagination. For you we have created the Bleeding Edge™ Group.

We're irreverent yet highly effective. We are very serious and focused, yet we laugh and know how to have a good time. We push the limits. We make ourselves vulnerable and humble so that we are ready to learn at extreme speed. We recognize that "look" others give when you have yet another idea. We are respectful and compassionate. We know what it means to live in the extreme.

When you need to perform in Extreme Business, you don't have the time or energy to mess around. All Bleeding Edge products and services are labeled with a skull and crossbones. The warning is clear– ☠ USE AT YOUR OWN RISK You can count on focused, hard-hitting, effective methodology, delivered with humor and irreverence. Right to the point—what you see is what you get.